Hamlyn nature guides
Wild flowers

Hamlyn
London · New York · Sydney · Toronto

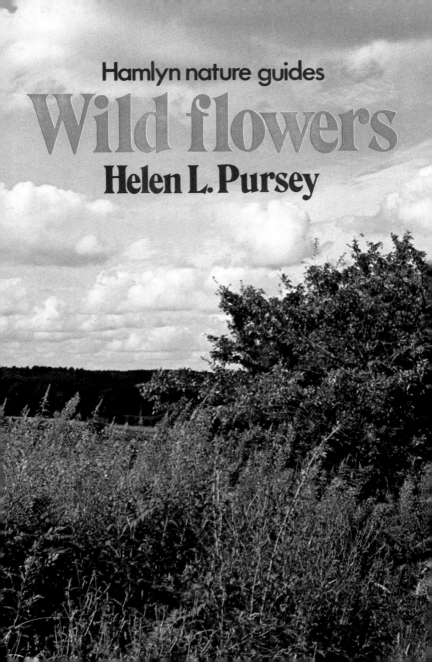

Hamlyn nature guides

Wild flowers

Helen L. Pursey

Acknowledgements

D. AICHELE: 52L, 111L; H. ANGEL: back jacket, 14R, 31L, 35R, ·38R, 41L, 43L, 45R, 47R, 49L, 50L, 51R, 54L, 55R, 56R, 68R, 73L, 75R, 81R, 95L, 100L, 101R, 106R, 107R, 108R, 109L, 114R, 118L, 122L, 123L; AQUILA PHOTOGRAPHICS: A. J. Bond 86R, A. W. Cundall 78R; ARDEA PHOTOGRAPHICS: J. R. Beames 39R, 64R, 76R, A. & E. Bomford 53R, S. Gooders 29L, 63L, 98L, J. Mason 28L, 120L; BRUCE COLEMAN LTD: J. & D. Bartlett 54R, S. C. Bisserot 70R, 119R, J. Burton 95R, 106L, 110L, A. J. Deane 48R, J. Markham 25L + R, 31R, 44R, 62L, 71R, 116L, R. K. Murton 60L, S. C. Porter 105R, 121R, S. Prato 37L, 42R, 51L, 91L, M. P. Price 89R, H. Reinhard 21L, 22L, 36R, 45L, 60R, 62R, 83R, 84R, 85L, 93R, 117L, 119L, 122R, U. Schneiders 113L, D. Washington 123R; J. CROSS: 67R; N. CURTIS 69L; W. F. DAVIDSON: title page, 24L, 26L, 27L, 46R, 77L, 91R, 93L, 107L, 110R; E. A. ELLIS: 18R; R. FLETCHER: front jacket; G. FRY: 97L; JACANA: H. Chaumeton 48L, L. Lacoste 57L, C. Nardin 17L, 37R, 78L, 83L, J. L. Reichmann 90R, G. Sommer 14L, M. Viard 96R; A. JUNG 20L; G. JURITZA: 57R; P. KOHLHAUPT: 121L; H. LACEY: 92L, 102L; H. R. LOWES: 34R, 77R, 114L; NATURAL HISTORY PHOTOGRAPHIC AGENCY: T. A. Cope 23L, S. Dalton 34L, 49R, 50R, 66R, 69R, 74L, 98R, 108L, 115L, 121L, H. & C. Foord 15R, 16L + R, 17R, 18L, 19L + R, 20R, 24R, 33L, 35L, 39L, 41R, 43R, 61R, 63R, 68L, 72L, 74R, 75L, 80L + R, 81L, 82L, 88L, 94R, 96L, 111R, 117R, B. Hawkes 40L, 55L, 71L, G. E. Hyde 26R, 27L, 28R, 29R, 30L + R, 32L + R, 36L, 38L, 40R, 52R, 53L, 58L + R, 59L, 61L, 64L, 65L + R, 66L, 70L, 72R, 76L, 79L + R, 82R, 85R, 86L, 88R, 89L, 90L, 94L, 97L, 99L + R, 100R, 101L, 102R, 103L + R, 104L, 105L, 109R, 112R, 113R, 115R, 116R, 120R, E. A. Janes 15L, 23R, 59R, 67L, 118R, J. Jeffrey 73R, K. G. Preston-Mafham 46L, 47L, 92R, 104R; H. OLDROYD 42L, 56L, 84L; H. SCHREMPP 22R, 33R; F. SCHWABLE: 21R, 87R; M. W. STOREY 44L, 87L.

Published by The Hamlyn Publishing Group Limited
London · New York · Sydney · Toronto
Astronaut House, Feltham, Middlesex, England
Copyright © The Hamlyn Publishing Group Limited 1978
Reprinted 1978,1979
ISBN 0 600 39381 X

Phototypeset by Tradespools Limited, Frome, Somerset
Printed in Italy

Contents

Introduction
Wild plants and Man

From earliest times man has been interested in plants and animals. Early cave-dwellers have left records of the animals they knew as, for example, in the famous cave paintings at Lascaux in central France. During the times of the Pharaohs, the Egyptians depicted plants, and domestic and other animals, in their temples. For several thousand years man has used plants for medicinal purposes and, even today, despite the chemical synthesis of many modern drugs, medicinal plants are widely used in the drug industry.

One of the more interesting and pleasing facets of modern times is the increasing concern shown by layman and specialist alike for wildlife and conservation generally. Much of this interest has been stimulated by travel and nature films, radio and television programmes, as well as articles in newspapers and magazines. There is a growing awareness that not only are rare species of plants and wild animals threatened by various changes in the environment but that this may apply even to common species.

Such changes include the construction of airports, new towns, factories, and housing estates which may in turn result in a demand for additional roadways, sewage works, and water supplies. Modern methods of farming require larger fields within which to manoeuvre bulky machinery, so that hedgerows are destroyed. In addition, chemical fertilizers and toxic sprays against weeds and insect pests may be spread on the soil and crops and, when washed out of the soil, may lead to serious pollution of nearby rivers. Atmospheric pollution is mainly due to waste gases in factory smoke and car exhausts and this can also be a menace to plant and animal life. Not all such changes are totally destructive, however; thus, motorway verges can form miniature nature reserves for plants and animals and new reservoirs may rapidly be colonized by waterfowl.

Many people are interested in plants and animals which, because of their beauty and intriguing variety, appeal to photographers, walkers, cyclists, and motorists. This interest is often extended to the wildlife of other countries. Nowadays, it is realized that it is better to observe and record rather than to collect and possibly destroy. This book seeks to encourage those who are looking at the beauty of flowers and attempting, possibly for the first time, to identify the specimens they find.

How to use this book

It is suggested that you use the following method:

Check (1) flower colour;
(2) number, size, and shape of petals;
(3) are the petals separate or joined (even if only slightly)?
(4) flower shape, whether radially or bilaterally symmetrical;
(5) is it really a flowerhead consisting of many small florets?

Then refer to the appropriate colour section; the sections are arranged with white flowers first, then green, red, pink, purple, blue, brown, yellow, and finally bicoloured flowers. Compare the flower with the photographs: it may be necessary to check with other colour sections because the flower colour can vary. Plants which have separate petals and are radially symmetrical (that is, star- or cross-shaped) will be found towards the beginning of each section.

Before completing the identification, confirm by checking time of flowering, shape and general appearance of the leaves, size and form of the plant, and the habitat. Never attempt an identification by leaves alone.

In the flower descriptions, technical terms have been kept to a minimum without sacrificing scientific accuracy. A short glossary of terms has been provided at the end of the book. The metric system of measurement has been used throughout this book but please note that metre has been abbreviated to m, the centimetre to cm, and the millimetre to mm.

Plant names

Common and scientific names of the plants have been given. Where possible, it is preferable to use the scientific name because this is international, whereas the common name may vary from country to country and sometimes even in different parts of the same country. The scientific name is in two parts, the first name being that of the genus (which can be likened to a surname) and the second that of the species (which corresponds to a forename or Christian name). Most genera have a number of different species. The specific name is often very informative, for example, *alba* indicates white, *perennis* shows that the plant lives for several years, *maritimum* that it lives by the sea.

Parts of a plant
The leaves

In some plants the leaves are more conspicuous than the flowers. Leaves differ markedly in size and shape yet they can be classed into a few basic types. Thus, plants in the major group, monocotyledons, usually have strap- or sword-shaped leaves with a number of parallel veins. This contrasts with the other major group, dicotyledons, which has mostly net-veined leaves of varying shape.

Undivided leaves are termed simple and may, for example, be long and narrow, oval, heart-shaped, or broad and lobed, but never divided into separate segments or leaflets (Fig. 1). Compound leaves are always divided into distinct leaflets and are either palmate, with the leaflets radiating from a common point, or pinnate with leaflets borne on each side of a common axis. The leaflets are sometimes still further subdivided (dissected) so that they appear almost feathery. To distinguish between a leaf and a leaflet, examine the base of the structure, if necessary, using a hand-lens. A leaf always has a bud at its base (however tiny) but a leaflet does not. Simple leaves may be palmately or pinnately lobed and both compound and simple leaves may have margins which are either smooth or indented.

At the base of some leaves a pair of outgrowths may be seen. These are stipules and they are characteristic of some flower families such as Rosaceae and Papilionaceae. They vary in shape and function and may be leafy or modified into tendrils or spines. Tendrils are often developed by climbing plants and are commonly, although not always, modified leaves or leaflets. They are highly sensitive to touch and quickly coil round the stems or other parts of nearby plants. Tendrils are particularly common in the pea family (Papilionaceae).·

Fig 1

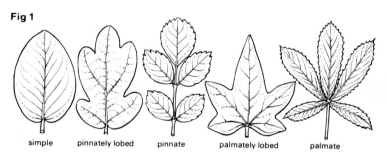

| simple | pinnately lobed | pinnate | palmately lobed | palmate |

The flower and its function

Somewhat surprisingly, the flower itself is thought to consist of a series of specially modified leaves. If we examine a relatively simple flower such as the buttercup (*Ranunculus*) we can see the various parts quite clearly (Fig. 2a). At the outside of the flower is a whorl of five, green sepals. These are obviously leaf-like in appearance and, although small, serve to protect the flower in bud. Within the sepals are five bright-yellow, glossy petals; these are also leaf-like in shape but, being brightly coloured, are attractive to insect visitors. The numerous, small, yellow stamens and ovary in the centre of the flower have no

Fig 2a Goldilocks Buttercup
(*Ranunculus auricomus*)

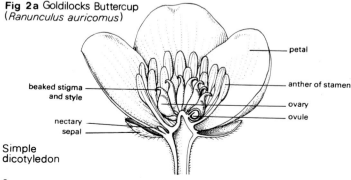

beaked stigma and style

nectary

sepal

petal

anther of stamen

ovary

ovule

Simple
dicotyledon

easily recognizable leaf-like features. The stamens contain pollen and the ovary contains the ovules which will subsequently develop into seeds. For seeds to be produced the ovules must be fertilized; pollen is transferred to the receptive stigmas of the ovary and there germinates, putting out a long pollen tube down into the ovary.

These four different kinds of flower parts are typical of flowers in the dicotyledons. In monocotyledons there is no obvious distinction into sepals and petals.

Pollination Insects, including a variety of flies and bees, visit flowers such as buttercups for pollen or nectar and accidentally brush pollen from the fertile anthers on to the stigmas; this is an example of insect pollination. More specialized flowers such as those of the families Papilionaceae, Labiatae, and Scrophulariaceae usually require long-tongued insects for successful pollination. The flowers of these and some other families are irregular, that is, they can be cut into equal halves in only one plane, from front to back of the flower. A good example is the Sweet Pea (*Lathyrus odoratus*) with its pronounced standard at the back of the flower (Fig. 2b), the wings at each side serving as an alighting platform for insect visitors, and the partly hidden keel (formed from two small, joined petals) protecting the stamens and ovary.

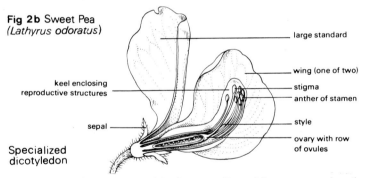

Fig 2b Sweet Pea
(*Lathyrus odoratus*)

large standard

wing (one of two)

keel enclosing reproductive structures

stigma

anther of stamen

sepal

style

ovary with row of ovules

Specialized dicotyledon

A somewhat small group of the insect-pollinated flowers comprises those visited by flies. These flowers tend to be sombre in colour, purplish or greenish, as in the figwort (*Scrophularia*) and with a nauseating odour (rather like that of rotting flesh) highly attractive to many flies.

Specialized flowers tend to have small numbers of flower parts (fours or fives in the dicotyledons, threes in the monocotyledons) with some, if not all, of the parts joined to one another. This fusion of parts is most obvious in the corolla, and results in a variety of shapes, some of which are typical of a particular family. One of the clearest examples is seen in the family, Labiatae; here, the five members of the corolla are joined to form a tube which expands above the throat to form the characteristic two-lipped corolla. The upper lip is frequently arched and hides the stamens and style, the lower lip is spreading with three well-defined lobes.

By contrast, the corolla of the family, Scrophulariaceae, although also formed from five fused petals, is extremely variable in shape. Thus, the mullein (*Verbascum*) has such a short tube that the corolla lobes look like five separate petals and in the speedwell (*Veronica*), the corolla appears to consist of four distinct petals. In the foxglove (*Digitalis*), the corolla takes the form of a long, thimble-shaped tube with a slightly lobed margin. In the snapdragon (*Antirrhinum*) the tubular corolla is strongly two-lipped with a basal pouch, the lower lip having a 'hump' which closes the throat of the flower; such a shape requires considerable pressure for a visiting insect to effect an entry, and it is not surprising to find that bumble-bees are the only pollinating insects for this flower. The toadflax (*Linaria*) has a corolla similar in shape to that of the snapdragon but smaller and with a long, nectar-containing spur. These examples are but a few of the varied corolla shapes found in one family, all being built up from the basic structure of five fused petals.

Specialized or advanced flowers also commonly bear the flower parts on top of the ovary, whereas in simple flowers, such as the buttercup, the sepals, petals, and stamens originate below the ovary. One of the most highly specialized monocotyledon families is that of the orchids (Fig. 2c), some of the flowers bearing a fancied or real resemblance to a variety of animals. The Compositae are the most specialized and successful of the dicotyledons with small florets clustered together to form an often large and attractive 'flower' much visited by a wide range of insects and which sets copious seed.

Insects are not the only pollinating agents. Many flowers are pollinated by the wind blowing clouds of dust-like pollen from the stamens on to feathery stigmas. Examples of this method include the Hop (*Humulus lupulus*) and Stinging Nettle (*Urtica dioica*) as well as grasses, sedges, and catkin-bearing trees. Such flowers are characterized by an absence of petals which prevents wastage of pollen; also the flowers and, in particular, the stamens, usually dangle on long, slender stalks, a device which facilitates easy dispersal of the pollen. Less common pollinating agents include birds, bats, snails, and even water, and the flowers concerned again show special adaptations. Flower structure tends to favour cross-pollination as it usually results in more vigorous progeny although self-pollination can and does occur.

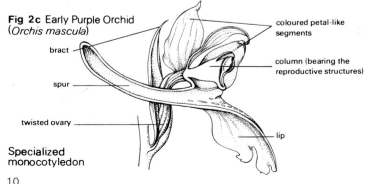

Fig 2c Early Purple Orchid (*Orchis mascula*)

coloured petal-like segments

bract

column (bearing the reproductive structures)

spur

twisted ovary

lip

Specialized monocotyledon

Fig 2d *Scilla campanulata*

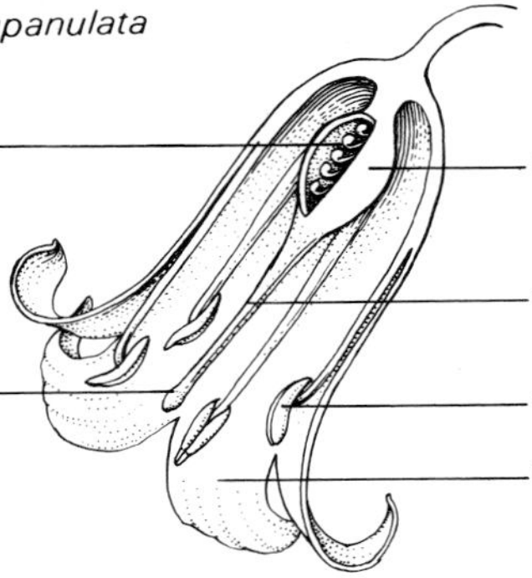

ovule — ovary

— style

stigma — anther of stamen

— joined petal-like segments

Simple
monocotyledon

Fertilization Pollination is followed by fertilization of the ovules; the ovary now begins to develop into a fruit and its mature form will depend on the original form of the ovary. Looking again at the buttercup flower, the ovary in the centre consists of a dome-shaped axis bearing numerous slightly beaked structures, each with its own stigma and enclosed ovule. The resultant buttercup fruits consist of a number of small, single-seeded nutlets each of which can drop off and eventually produce a new plant.

The fruit

Nuts and nutlets are *dry* fruits having a hard or papery coat which is eventually broken or rotted away allowing the seed to germinate. Other dry fruits may be pods or rounded capsules which open in a precise way by slits, pores, teeth, or lids releasing the often numerous seeds.

Fleshy fruits have a succulent fruit wall which is coloured and attractive to birds and other animals. The berry is a fleshy fruit with numerous, hard-coated seeds, for example, honeysuckle (*Lonicera*) and currant (*Ribes*), whereas the drupe, such as in the cherry and plum (*Prunus*), contains only one seed enclosed within the hard stone. The familiar blackberry is a collection of small drupelets. Some fleshy fruits are composite structures with other flower parts developing outside the ovary to form the mature fruit. Such fruits are called *false* fruits and they include the strawberry (*Fragaria*), Crab Apple (*Malus sylvestris*) and the familiar rosehip.

Dispersal of fruit The dispersal of fruits and seeds is one of the most fascinating aspects of plant reproduction. Fleshy fruits are almost always eaten by birds and other animals, the seeds ultimately being excreted in the droppings some distance away from the parent plant. Far from being harmed by their passage through the gut, most of the seeds germinate more freely, probably because their hard coats are abraded and water uptake can then take place more readily.

The greatest variety of dispersal mechanisms is shown by dry fruits. Nuts and nutlets are an important item of food for many small animals and may be eaten on the spot or carried away, as in the well-known winter hoards of the squirrel. Other dry fruits may open, the seeds then being shaken out or falling directly to the ground. The poppy capsule has a number of small pores under the flat-topped head; when the stalk sways, the minute seeds are shaken out —this is known as a 'censer mechanism'. The exposed seeds of other dry fruits may be carried away for food by ants, birds, and other animals. Some fruits are borne away attached to fur, feathers or even clothing and, if picked off and examined, will be seen to be armed with various forms of hooks or bristles. Such 'burr fruits' are quite common and include those of burdock (*Arctium*) and goosegrass (*Galium*).

The wind may also act as a dispersal agent, blowing away tiny, dust-like seeds such as those of the orchids, or wafting away hairy or cottony seeds such as those of willowherb (*Epilobium*) and Red Valerian (*Centranthus ruber*). Whole fruits may also be dispersed by the wind, probably the best known examples being the plumed nutlets of the dandelion 'clock' and the propeller-like fruits of the sycamore and maple (*Acer*). Perhaps the most fascinating fruits are those which actively discharge their seeds explosively, the mechanism depending on a build-up of tension as the fruit wall ripens. Explosive fruits may be relatively simple in structure as in gorse pods which, on a hot summer day, suddenly split into two and eject the seeds, or more complex as in the long-beaked fruit of the cranesbill (*Geranium*): the five one-seeded nutlets suddenly separate and coil upwards, throwing out the seeds. Even more curious is the mainly Mediterranean Squirting Cucumber (*Ecballium elaterium*) with its greenish, fleshy fruits which drop to the ground when ripe, violently discharging a stream of seeds and liquid through the hole at the stalk end of the fruit.

The dispersal of fruits and seeds away from the parent plant is extremely important, reducing overcrowding and, therefore, competition between plants for light, air, and moisture. It also enables the plant to colonize other areas. One particularly interesting aspect of seeds is the ability of many kinds to remain dormant during periods when conditions are unsuitable for germination. Authenticated records are known of seeds which have germinated successfully after a period of one to several hundred years. Less dramatically, land which is dug over or deep-ploughed usually produces a crop of weeds although there may formerly have been no evidence of them. It is only when long-buried seeds are brought to the surface that conditions suitable for germination are encountered. This phenomenon is an example of dispersal in time and it may play a very important part in the life of plants.

Plant ecology

Weeds are common and highly successful plants, able to live in a wide range of habitats because their requirements are unspecialized. All plants need light, air and soil, adequate moisture, and a suitable temperature for successful growth. Many plants, however, appear to have special requirements which limit or exclude them from some habitats although enabling them to be highly successful in others. Thus, some plants can thrive only in a limy or chalky soil, while others require the acid soil of heath or moorland. Some plants need full sun whereas others tolerate dense woodland shade. It will be obvious, therefore, that although seeds may be dispersed over a wide area, there may not necessarily be any increase in the number and spread of new plants.

The study of particular plants in a given habitat and of the associated plants which together form a 'community', is known as plant ecology. Broadly speaking the following types of habitat can be distinguished and each can be further subdivided. Usually, certain plants are characteristic of particular habitats and may, indeed, be so abundant that they are said to be dominant.

Some important habitats are described briefly below.

Woodland – deciduous or evergreen (conifer) – usually has three layers of vegetation, that is, tree layer, shrub layer, and the ground flora.

Scrub (including hedgerows) is an intermediate stage between grassland and woodland.

Heath, Moor, and Mountain – heath and moorland develop on acid soils with heaths (*Erica*) and Heather (*Calluna vulgaris*) as dominant plants. Moorland develops at higher altitudes and is, therefore, characteristic of low mountain slopes. Mountain-dwelling plants, that is, those living at higher altitudes among rocks and on stony screes are known as alpines and may be small and often cushion-like in habit.

Grassland is actually of three main types depending on the amount of lime in the soil: acid, neutral, and calcareous, each with its own particular flora. Acid grassland shades into heath and has fewer flower species; neutral grassland is mostly agricultural in use and origin but has a number of flower species. Some of these are also found in calcareous grassland which is characteristic of chalk and limestone areas and is rich in species, particularly of orchids.

Waste and Cultivated Ground is essentially bare ground which, if not deliberately planted, ultimately becomes colonized by more or less familiar weeds of various kinds. Paths, roadsides, and walls are also included here.

Aquatic habitats are of two kinds: MARITIME, that is, coastal habitats including salt marshes, sand dunes and shingle, and sea cliffs; FRESHWATER, that is, lakes and ponds, rivers, streams, and ditches – in all of which there is normally abundant water – and habitats with a lower level of standing water such as swamps and marshes, bogs and fens. Bogs develop on acid soils whereas fens usually develop on neutral or calcareous soils. Aquatic plants may live more or less submerged, or may grow at the water surface, or may simply root in wet soil.

With practice, you can quickly assess a particular habitat and make a reasonable forecast of the plants most likely to be found there. Most of these will be common, some will be specialized and a few may even be rare. Never pick rare flowers or, even worse, dig them up. They are unlikely to survive being transplanted whereas, if left where they are growing, they may seed and increase, continuing to give pleasure to other people.

Family Ranunculaceae

Wood Anemone

Anemone nemorosa

March–May. Attractive white flowers (rarely lilac or pale blue), flushed pink or purplish below; each flower is solitary, about 3cm across, with six or seven (sometimes more) petal-like segments surrounding a central mass of yellow stamens; much visited by bees and certain flies for pollen.

Form of plant the slender flower stems, up to 30cm high, bear three three-lobed leaves about two-thirds up from the base forming a characteristic 'frill' below each flower; later one or two similar leaves develop at ground level; perennial.

Habitat open woodlands, hedgebanks, and sometimes mountain meadows on most soils except the very acid or water logged; always in large numbers forming carpets.

Distribution common throughout most of Europe except the extreme north and south.

Family Nymphaeaceae

White Water-lily

Nymphaea alba

June–September. Large, showy, and fragrant, many-petalled flowers which rise to the surface of the water under the influence of light, open only in sunshine, closing and sinking beneath the water towards evening; outside the narrow petals are four green sepals lined with white; within the petals are numerous stamens and an ovary with a yellow disc of fourteen to twenty stigmas; the fruit ripens under water and bursts open to release many buoyant air-filled seeds.

Form of plant an aquatic plant rooted in the mud beneath the water; all leaves are large, floating and almost circular, with stalks up to 3m long, the lower leaf-surface often reddish; perennial.

Habitat still, shallow lakes and ponds; up to 1600m.

Distribution almost throughout Europe.

14

Family Cruciferae

Garlic Mustard

Alliaria petiolata

April–July. Small flowers with four petals typically arranged in a cross; borne at the top of the stems in a leafless cluster which later extends to form a spike; fruits are roughly cylindrical pods about 6cm long on short sturdy stalks.

Form of plant erect unbranched slightly hairy stems 20–120cm high; leaves thin, wrinkled, and light green, roughly heart-shaped with deeply toothed edges; strong odour of garlic when crushed; biennial.

Habitat hedgerows and shady waysides, shaded gardens, and at the bases of walls, often in groups; also in open woodland on limy soils.

Distribution common throughout northern Europe but becoming less common in the extreme south.

Hairy Rockcress

Arabis hirsuta

May–August. Numerous small flowers, 3–5mm across, in a long, rather dense spike; each flower with four petals, typically arranged in a cross; the four sepals often purple with a white margin, alternating with the petals; fruits short-stalked slender pods up to 5cm long, erect and close to the flower stem.

Form of plant very variable; one or more upright and usually unbranched, rough, hairy flower stems up to 60cm high; they arise from a basal rosette of hairy, spoon-shaped leaves 22cm long (sometimes longer); stem leaves also hairy but shorter and erect, clasping the stem; biennial or short-lived perennial.

Habitat chalk and limestone rocks, walls and hill slopes, hedgebanks, dry chalk grassland, and sand dunes.

Distribution fairly common throughout most of Europe.

Shepherd's Purse

Capsella bursa-pastoris

January–December. Tiny flowers, with the four petals typical of the family, growing in long rather flat-topped flowerheads; flowers generally produced throughout the year, self-pollinated; the small fruits are heart-shaped, resembling a miniature purse, thus giving rise to the common name.

Form of plant extremely variable in size and leaf form; stems between 3 and 40cm high, growing from a rosette of elongate leaves which may be pinnately notched or sometimes undivided; the upper leaves are arrow-shaped and clasp the stems; annual or biennial.

Habitat waste places, by waysides and on cultivated land of all kinds.

Distribution common throughout Europe and in almost every other part of the world.

Common Scurvy-grass

Cochlearia officinalis

April–August. Scented, four-petalled flowers (sometimes lilac) 8–10mm across in flat-topped clusters which elongate as the fruits develop; insect visitors are chiefly flies and beetles; the fruits are almost globular and about 6mm across.

Form of plant a smooth somewhat fleshy herb with several stems up to 50cm high; basal leaves forming a loose rosette, each leaf kidney- or heart-shaped and long stalked; upper leaves toothed or lobed, without stalks and clasping the stem; very variable in size, degree of fleshiness, and shape of fruits; biennial or perennial, rarely annual.

Habitat salt marshes, sea walls, and cliffs; essentially a maritime plant although sometimes found in mountainous areas inland.

Distribution widely distributed in northern, western, and central Europe.

Seakale

Crambe maritima

May-August. Sweet-scented, characteristically four-petalled flowers (sometimes reddish) in many-branched, somewhat flat-topped clusters which may reach 30cm across; the flower petals are 6–9mm long and, if pulled apart, are green at the base; the fruits are globular and are dispersed by the tides, the salt water having no harmful effect on the seed within.

Form of plant a distinctive bluish-green herb with erect stems up to 75cm high; leaves large, fleshy, and cabbage-like but rather more lobed; perennial.

Habitat seashores, often along the drift line on sand or shingle but also among rocks and on cliffs.

Distribution somewhat uncommon, but found along the Baltic, Atlantic, and Black Sea coasts; not in the Mediterranean region.

Field Pepperwort

Lepidium campestre

May—August. Very small four-petalled flowers in long, cylindrical spikes borne terminally on the stem and branches; fruits are flattened and almost circular, characteristically covered with little white spots which later become scaly.

Form of plant an erect stem up to 60cm high, with upturned branches; the basal leaves fall before the flowers open, the middle and upper stem leaves are long and arrow-shaped, clasping the stem; leaves and stem appear blue-green because of a dense covering of hairs; annual or biennial.

Habitat dry fields and pastures, roadsides, walls, and waste places; up to 1500m or more.

Distribution not particularly common but found throughout Europe, rare in Scotland and Ireland.

Watercress

Nasturtium officinale

May–October. Leafless spikes of small four-petalled flowers about 5mm across, the petals nearly twice as long as the sepals; visited by flies and small bees; fruit a pod 13–18mm long.

Form of plant a small aquatic herb with light-green stems and darker leaves which remain green throughout the winter; the stems grow up to 60cm long and produce tufts of white roots on the lower parts; leaves pinnately divided with five to nine (or more) rather glossy rounded leaflets; perennial.

Habitat streams and ditches or on nearby mud; never in still or acid waters; cultivated for salad in special beds in shallow streams.

Distribution common throughout southern and central Europe as far north as Britain and southern Sweden.

Wild Radish

Raphanus raphanistrum

May–September. Open spikes of dainty four-petalled flowers which vary considerably in colour including yellow, mauve, or violet; each flower about 2cm across, the white and yellow forms delicately veined with purple; fruits are beaked pods containing three to eight seeds, and have a noticeably beaded appearance, subsequently breaking into single-seeded segments.

Form of plant an exceedingly bristly herb with a branched or unbranched leafy stem 20–60cm high; the lower leaves deeply pinnately lobed with a large rounded terminal lobe, upper leaves smaller and less deeply cut; annual.

Habitat cultivated fields, bare and waste ground, especially on acid soils; a common and troublesome weed.

Distribution found throughout Europe but introduced (not native) in the extreme north.

Family Caryophyllaceae

Field Pennycress

Thlaspi arvense

May—September. Tiny four-petalled flowers in long spikes, the fruits developing quickly so that, as in other members of the family, young flowers and ripe fruits grow in the same spike; each fruit is an almost circular pod 10—18mm across, with a broad wing each side and deeply notched at the top.

Form of plant a small, erect herb, 10—60cm high, with toothed leaves; basal leaves oval, the stem leaves long and arrow-shaped, partly clasping the stem; leaves emitting an offensive odour when crushed; annual.

Habitat cultivated fields and waste places; sometimes a troublesome weed.

Distribution found in most of Europe but not in the Mediterranean region and rare in the extreme north.

Thyme-leaved Sandwort

Arenaria serpyllifolia

April—November. Small flowers, up to 8mm across, in forked groupings made up of only a few flowers; each flower with five sepals and petals, the sepals slender and twice as long as the petals; usually ten yellowish stamens; fruit small and flask-shaped, opening by six short teeth.

Form of plant a rather bushy little herb with slender grey-green stems varying between 2·5 and 25cm high; leaves tiny, oval, and pointed and covered with small, rough hairs; annual (sometimes biennial).

Habitat dry, usually sandy places including walls, bare ground and open fields, cliff tops; rabbits tend to avoid it so that it is often common around their burrows.

Distribution common throughout Europe except in the extreme north.

19

Common Mouse-ear Chickweed

Cerastium fontanum

April—November. Small flowers about 8mm across grow in open, branched groupings, each flower with five deeply notched petals not much longer than the sepals.

Form of plant very variable, but is generally a low-growing herb with many sprawling, leafy, hairy stems some of which grow upright to 45cm and flower; leaves about 2·5cm long, oval and paired, dark greyish green in colour with a dense, white, hairy coating; plants from upland areas are smaller and more hairy but have larger flowers.

Habitat waste and cultivated ground, shingle and sand dunes, also grassland.

Distribution exceedingly common, found throughout Europe and, indeed, in most parts of the world, in both lowland and upland regions.

Common Pearlwort

Sagina procumbens

May—October. Minute, insignificant flowers 5—7mm across, borne singly on upright stalks 5—20mm long; flower parts in fours, sometimes fives; the white, sometimes yellowish, petals are much shorter than the sepals, and may be missing altogether.

Form of plant a tufted mat with a dense central rosette of leaves and many prostrate, rooting and leafy, lateral stems up to 20cm long; leaves paired, 5—12mm long, needle-like and ending in a fine, hair-like point; rather variable; perennial.

Habitat damp, bare soils and short, grassy places including paths, lawns, banks, and stream sides; in lowland and upland areas up to 1500m or more.

Distribution common, and found throughout Europe.

Bladder Campion

Silene vulgaris

April—September. Drooping, white, five-petalled flowers easily recognized by the swollen, almost papery looking calyx, pale green or purplish, with a network of main and subsidiary veins; petals deeply cleft but the scales at the throat of the flower hardly noticeable; flowers fragrant and attractive to long-tongued bees and night-flying moths.

Form of plant several upright, leafy stems, all with flowers, growing up to 90cm high; the paired leaves are lance-shaped and, like the stems, may be smooth or hairy; very variable, with a number of subspecies; perennial.

Habitat roadsides, waste, cultivated, and grassy places, rocks and screes; from the sea coast to inland mountain regions, depending on the subspecies.

Distribution common throughout most of Europe.

Corn Spurrey

Spergula arvensis

May—September. Dainty, star-like, five-petalled flowers in a well-spaced, forking spike, the developing fruits on downward-pointing stalks giving the whole spike a curious, somewhat zig-zag appearance; flowers 4—7mm across; seeds often winged.

Form of plant a small greyish- or grass-green herb with delicate, jointed, and branched stems 7·5—40cm high; leaves in clusters, each leaf needle-shaped, about 3cm long, and with tiny, chaffy stipules; stems and leaves usually sticky with glandular hairs; very variable in colour and hairiness; annual.

Habitat cornfields and other cultivated ground, especially on sandy and gravelly soils, never on chalk or limestone; often a troublesome weed.

Distribution almost cosmopolitan, being found throughout Europe and much of the world; locally abundant.

Greater Stitchwort

Stellaria holostea

April—June. Conspicuous star-like flowers in forked, open groups; each flower is 15—30mm across and has five petals which are twice as long as the sepals; the petals are usually split into two half way but are sometimes further subdivided, occasionally completely missing.

Form of plant light-green leafy stems, some non-flowering and short, the flowering stems reaching 60cm; all stems upright but spindly and tending to lean against other plants; the leaves are paired, stiff, and narrow, tapering to a long point, and with rough edges and midrib under-surface; perennial.

Habitat hedgerows, thickets, and open woods; in lowland and hilly areas.

Distribution common in much of Europe but rare in the Mediterranean region.

Chickweed

Stellaria media

January—December. Small, white flowers about 1cm across, the five petals split so deeply that they look like ten but sometimes absent altogether; three to ten stamens with red-purple anthers.

Form of plant a familiar little herb with sprawling, branched, leafy stems usually up to 40cm, but sometimes twice as long; the leaves are small and hairless, oval and paired, the stem between each leaf pair characteristically with a single line of hairs which alternates from side to side of the stem; extremely variable in size, leaf, and flower characteristics; annual or overwintering.

Habitat roadsides, cultivated and waste ground; an extremely common weed; up to 2500m.

Distribution cosmopolitan, being found in most parts of the world.

Family Portulacaceae

Perfoliate Claytonia

Montia perfoliata

April–July. Small, long-stalked, star-like flowers 5–8mm across, loosely clustered within a wide green collar (involucre) formed by the upper leaves; pollinated by various small insects; the fruits are small capsules containing one to three shiny black seeds.

Form of plant a noticeably smooth, fleshy herb with a rosette of long-stalked, oval basal leaves, and one or more upright flowering stems 10–30cm high; at the top of each stem is a single pair of leaves which join to form the characteristic encircling involucre; annual.

Habitat cultivated and waste ground, especially on rather dry sandy soils.

Distribution sometimes locally abundant; actually a native of North America, and has become naturalized in western Europe, including Britain.

Family Oxalidaceae

Common Wood Sorrel

Oxalis acetosella

April–July. Dainty, pendant, five-petalled flowers, 2–3cm across, usually white (sometimes pink or purple) with purple veins; flowers solitary on slender stalks 5–15cm high with two small bracts half way; most flowers remain unpollinated but later in the summer insignificant non-opening flowers set seed; the fruits split open and the seeds are explosively discharged.

Form of plant a low-growing, pale-green herb with long-stalked, clover-like leaves; the leaflets droop and fold together at night; perennial.

Habitat woods, hedgebanks, shady rocks; often growing in moss or rotting leaves and frequently in deep shade; commonly forming a carpet on the floor of oak or beech woods; up to 2120m.

Distribution common in most of Europe, rarer in the south.

23

Family Rosaceae

Meadowsweet

Filipendula ulmaria

June—September. Tiny, highly fragrant, creamy white flowers crowded into large irregular and branched clusters; each flower is five-petalled with numerous stamens and is attractive to bees for its pollen.
Form of plant leafy, flowering stems up to 120cm high with handsome, toothed, pinnate leaves in which pairs of small leaflets alternate with large ones, the terminal leaflet being large and three-lobed; the lower leaf surface is white with downy hairs, the upper surface dark green and hairless; perennial.
Habitat found in a variety of moist situations such as river margins, marshes, damp meadows and woods, and also among damp rocks; found at up to 900m.
Distribution common throughout Europe except in the extreme south.

Family Crassulaceae

White Stonecrop

Sedum album

June—August. Numerous small, white, star-like flowers in a branched flat-topped flowerhead 2—5cm across, at first drooping but later becoming erect; flowers 6—9mm across, with five slender petals, often flushed pink beneath; the small fruitlets are also pink or reddish.
Form of plant mats of bare, creeping stems give rise to leafy, upright, flowering and non-flowering stems 5—18cm high; leaves bright green, smooth and fleshy, about 1cm long and more or less cylindrical in shape, densely crowded in the non-flowering shoots; stems and leaves often tinged with red; very variable; perennial.
Habitat old walls and roofs, rocky and gravelly places; up to 2500m.
Distribution not uncommon in much of Europe, probably naturalized in parts of the north and east.

Family Saxifragaceae
Meadow Saxifrage
Saxifraga granulata

April—June. Dainty, star-like, five-petalled flowers, 2—3cm across, borne in open clusters on a flower stem up to 50cm high.

Form of plant a small herb with hairy stem and leaves; stem leaves few or none, basal leaves fleshy, broadly lobed and kidney-shaped, in a rosette which soon withers; small, brown, egg-shaped bodies (bulbils), about 5mm across, enable the plant to overwinter and can also form new plants; very variable in size, form and type of habitat; perennial.

Habitat well-drained glassland, also dry rocky places; some varieties of plant preferring acid soils, others on limy soils; lowland and upland forms, to 2170m.

Distribution not common but found throughout much of Europe.

Family Droseraceae
Common Sundew
Drosera rotundifolia

June—August. Insignificant five-petalled flowers arranged to one side of a coiled flowering stem; the flowers open only in sunny weather.

Form of plant an unusual and intriguing plant; the small, round, long-stalked leaves form a rosette, each leaf bearing long, red, glandular hairs ('tentacles') which each has a globule of sticky, glistening fluid at its tip; these droplets are attractive to insects which alight and are held by the sticky fluid and then by the hairs which bend over; subsequently the leaf absorbs the softer parts of the insects; perennial.

Habitat wet, peaty places on heaths and moors, also peat bogs, up to 2000m.

Distribution common throughout Europe except in the Mediterranean region.

Family Onagraceae

Common Enchanter's Nightshade

Circaea lutetiana

June—September. Insignificant, long-stalked flowers widely spaced along the flower stem and with their parts in twos — red sepals, deeply notched white petals (sometimes pink) and pink stamens; fruits small and covered with white, hooked bristles which become entangled in fur or clothing helping to disperse the seeds.
Form of plant a single-stemmed herb reaching 70cm and bearing paired leaves up to 10cm long; these are oval with a tapering pointed tip and toothed edges, the lower surface is pale and shiny; stem and leaves bear soft hairs; perennial.
Habitat moist, often limy soils in woods and other shady places, sometimes an abundant garden weed.
Distribution common throughout Europe.

Family Umbelliferae

Fool's Parsley

Aethusa cynapium

June—October. Small white flowers arranged in compound umbels which are most easily recognized by the bracts at the outside; bracts long and slender, hanging downwards and looking rather like a frill; outer petals of the flowers slightly larger than the rest.
Form of plant very variable, with several subspecies; the stems are usually between 5 and 80cm high but may reach 200cm; leaves dark green and doubly pinnate, when young somewhat resembling parsley; poisonous and with a highly unpleasant odour; annual or biennial (depending on the subspecies).
Habitat essentially a weed of cultivated ground but a large subspecies is found in woodland.
Distribution common in most of Europe but rare in the Mediterranean region.

Wild Angelica

Angelica sylvestris

July—September. Minute flowers (sometimes pink) in large umbels (flowerheads) up to 15cm across made up of twenty to forty smaller umbels; when in bud the umbels are protected by large sheathing leaf bases; the small fruits bear papery wings.
Form of plant an extremely robust herb with hollow, grooved, purplish stems reaching 2m or more; the leaves are large (up to 60cm long) and pinnately subdivided but not feathery; perennial.
Habitat by streams, in fens and damp meadows and woods, but in upland areas it may be found in clearings and also stony places at up to 1780m.
Distribution common in most parts of Europe but more rare in the south.

Cow Parsley

Anthriscus sylvestris

April—June. A common, early flowering umbellifer with a number of terminal umbels of tiny flowers, the first-formed umbel becoming overtopped by the later ones; the outermost flowers in each umbel have petals slightly larger than the rest.
Form of plant hollow, furrowed stems up to 100cm high bear a number of large, much divided, rather feathery leaves; both stems and leaves are somewhat downy; rather variable in habit; biennial.
Habitat by roadsides, in hedgerows and at the margins of woodland, also in waste places.
Distribution common and widely distributed in north and central Europe but restricted to upland areas in southern Europe, becoming rare in Mediterranean regions.

Cowbane

Cicuta virosa

July—August. Small flowers in dense, long-stalked heads which are themselves grouped into radiating umbels; each umbel is flat topped and between 7 and 13cm across; all flower stalks within the umbel are distinctly reddish purple.

Form of plant a robust, erect plant up to 130cm tall; the stems are hollow and ridged and bear leaves up to 30cm long; each leaf is pinnately divided and the subdivisions are further pinnately divided; leaf stalks are hollow with a conspicuous sheathing base; all parts hairless and extremely poisonous if eaten; perennial.

Habitat ditches, marshes, and shallow water.

Distribution a rare plant of central and northern Europe.

Wild Carrot

Daucus carota

May—October. Minute flowers grouped in somewhat bowl-shaped umbels, about 7cm across, becoming noticeably concave when in fruit; the central flower (occasionally the central group of flowers) bright red or deep purple; the umbel surrounded by conspicuous feathery bracts hanging down below; fruits very bristly.

Form of plant somewhat variable but with a tough erect stem which may reach 100cm and which bears large feathery leaves; all parts very bristly and with the distinctive odour of the garden carrot; biennial.

Habitat fields, grassy places, roadsides, chiefly on chalky soils and particularly near the sea; a subspecies with narrower leaves and flat umbels is found among dunes and on cliffs.

Distribution common and widely distributed throughout Europe.

Hogweed

Heracleum sphondylium

April–November. Large, spreading, compound umbels (sometimes pinkish) reaching 20cm across with up to forty-five rays; the five-petalled flowers are 5–10mm across; outermost flowers with petals of unequal size, petals of all flowers deeply notched; fruits relatively large (up to 12mm long).

Form of plant a stout, erect herb with a hollow, ridged, hairy stem reaching 350cm high; leaves very large, pinnately divided into irregular segments roughly hairy above, densely covered with whitish hairs beneath; the leaf bases form large, strongly veined sheaths which protect the young leaves and flowers; biennial.

Habitat meadows, roadsides, hedgerows and woods; up to 2500m.

Distribution common in most of Europe except the far north and Mediterranean areas.

Burnet Saxifrage

Pimpinella saxifraga

May–October. Tiny flowers (rarely pinkish or purple) in small umbels which are clustered, six to twenty-five together, to form flat-topped, compound umbels up to 5cm across.

Form of plant a slender herbaceous plant with softly hairy somewhat ridged stems up to 100cm high; the long-stalked, pinnate basal leaves have three to seven pairs of toothed leaflets; the lower stem leaves are pinnate but much more subdivided, further up the stems the leaves become progressively smaller and simpler; leaf stalks of all leaves sheath-like and purplish; very variable in habit; perennial.

Habitat dry pastures and grassy places, roadsides and stony places, usually on limy soils; up to 2400m.

Distribution fairly common in most of Europe but absent from the extreme north and south.

Family Primulaceae

Chickweed Wintergreen

Trientalis europaea

May–August. Delicate star-like flowers, 11–19mm across, borne singly on long, hair-like stalks, usually one or two but sometimes up to four on a plant; each flower with five- to nine-pointed petals, occasionally tinged with pink.

Form of plant an attractive little herb with an upright, unbranched, leafy stem 5–30cm high; a few small leaves grow on the lower part of the stem but most form a whorl near the top, each leaf 1–9cm long, lance-shaped, stiff, and glossy; perennial.

Habitat damp, grassy places and pine woods, usually growing in moss and on acid, peaty soils; up to 2000m.

Distribution locally common in northern Europe, extending to the southern Alps; absent from southern Britain.

Family Boraginaceae

Common Gromwell

Lithospermum officinale

May–July. Insignificant, five-lobed, tubular greenish- or yellowish-white flowers, partly hidden by large leafy bracts, borne towards the upper end of stems and branches; the joined sepals persist until the fruits ripen, each fruit being a group of four, hard, glistening, white nutlets.

Form of plant an erect, much-branched herb, up to 100cm high, with undivided, long-pointed leaves; both stems and leaves are bristly to the touch; perennial.

Habitat hedges, thickets and other bushy places, also on waste land, not usually on acid soils; up to 2300m in mountain areas.

Distribution found in most of Europe but varying in frequency — never common — and rare in parts of the north and west.

Family Convolvulaceae

Convolvulus

Calystegia sepium

July—September. Conspicuous and handsome funnel-shaped flowers (sometimes pink) up to 7cm across, borne singly on four-sided stalks and with two large heart-shaped bracts at the base; the flowers have no scent and close at night.

Form of plant climbing stems up to 3m long which twine anticlockwise tightly around each other and around the stems of nearby plants; leaves widely spaced along the stems; each leaf about 15cm long, arrow- or heart-shaped and smooth; perennial.

Habitat hedgerows, scrub, and at the edges of woodland, in fens, and also in gardens where it can be a troublesome weed.

Distribution common throughout Europe except in the far north.

Family Solanaceae

Black Nightshade

Solanum nigrum

July—October. Drooping, sparsely flowered clusters of five-petalled flowers which have a central cone of yellow anthers, looking like a white form of Woody Nightshade but with berries that turn black when ripe.

Form of plant a branching herb with leafy, fairly upright stems not more than 70cm high; leaves up to 7cm long, often toothed and pointed, oval or diamond-shaped; annual.

Habitat waste places and cultivated soil, frequently a garden weed; in lowland and hilly areas up to 1740m.

Distribution growing in most of Europe but probably not a native plant in the north; in Britain it is fairly common but becoming far less so in northern counties; absent from most of Scotland.

Family Scrophulariaceae

Common Eyebright

Euphrasia officinalis

June–October. Small, open, two-lipped flowers, the lower lip larger and three-lobed, in terminal leafy clusters; flower colour (sometimes partly or wholly purple, rarely yellow) and size very variable but often with purple veins and a distinct yellow blotch on the lower lip.

Form of plant a short, tufted herb with hairy stems 5–25cm high and many small, deeply cut leaves; an extremely variable species which is usually subdivided; plants growing near the sea or in mountainous areas are less branched and have fleshy leaves; all plants are semiparasitic on grasses; annual.

Habitat moors, heaths, sea cliffs, coastal pastures, downs, meadows, and grassy mountain slopes.

Distribution some varieties common, others restricted and rare; found throughout Europe.

Family Acanthaceae

Bear's Breech

Acanthus mollis

May–August. Large, rather sombre flowers in imposing spiny, purplish-leaved spikes; flowers whitish with bronze-purple veins and of an unusual shape, the petals joined to form a tube with a large, three-lobed lower lip; pollinated by bumble-bees; fruits rounded, with two to four fairly large seeds which are ejected by means of tough but elastic seed stalks.

Form of plant an extremely robust herb with stout unbranched flower stems 100cm or more high; basal leaves large, handsome, and evergreen, up to 90cm long, arranged in a rosette; each leaf is a rich glossy green and deeply lobed; perennial.

Habitat roadsides and waste places, usually in shade.

Distribution native to central and western Europe, including Portugal, but naturalized in other areas including Britain.

Family Labiatae

Gipsywort

Lycopus europaeus

June—September. Insignificant, whitish flowers about 3mm across in crowded whorls along the stems, half hidden by the large deeply toothed leaves; the flowers are four-lobed and spotted with purple, producing a pinkish tint.

Form of plant an aquatic plant with scarcely branched four-angled stems up to 120cm high, with lance-shaped leaves 3—10cm or more long; stems and leaves often slightly hairy; the plant is completely odourless, unlike most members of the family; very variable in size, leaf form, and degree of hairiness; perennial.

Habitat the banks of ditches, streams and rivers, lake sides, marshes and fens, often among crowded vegetation.

Distribution widespread and usually common throughout Europe.

Catmint

Nepeta cataria

June—September. Small whitish flowers dotted with crimson (quite different from the garden Catmint) in dense leafy whorls along the stem and crowded together at the top so that it looks like a spike; each flower is two-lipped and about 12mm across.

Form of plant a strongly aromatic herb with branched, erect, four-angled stems up to 100cm high; the leaves are pointed, toothed, and more or less heart-shaped; the stems and the under-surfaces of the leaves are white with downy hairs; perennial.

Habitat waste ground, roadsides, hedgebanks, and rocky places; formerly cultivated as a medicinal plant and now widely naturalized.

Distribution not common but found in much of Europe from Scandinavia to the Mediterranean.

Family Rubiaceae

Hedge Bedstraw

Galium mollugo

June—September. Tiny, star-like flowers, each four-petalled and 2—3mm across, many together in rounded, much-branched clusters; pollinated chiefly by small flies; the fruits are small and wrinkled, turning black when dry.
Form of plant a straggling herb with weak, four-angled stems up to 150cm long; leaves light green, 8—25mm long, in whorls of six to eight along the stems; each leaf narrows at both ends and has a distinct bristle-tip, the leaf margins are rough with forward-pointing prickles; perennial.
Habitat meadows and grassy slopes, hedgebanks, open woodland and scrub, waste places, usually on chalky soils.
Distribution usually common, found throughout most of Europe except in the far north and some of the islands.

Family Compositae

Yarrow

Achillea millefolium

May—October. Minute flowers (sometimes pink or purplish) in small heads arranged in branched, flat-topped clusters about 8cm across borne terminally on the stems; at first sight could be confused with an umbellifer (which has obvious stamens in the centre of each flower); the flowers attract a great variety of insects.
Form of plant tough, upright, angular stems up to 60cm high, usually unbranched, with woolly, finely divided leaves about 12cm long; stems and leaves have a strong aromatic odour; perennial.
Habitat waste ground, waysides, hedgerows, and meadows on all but the poorest soils; in mountainous areas up to 3100m.
Distribution common virtually throughout Europe except for the far north.

Common Daisy

Bellis perennis

March—October, but all the year round in mild seasons. Small florets are grouped into the familiar daisy flower-heads (sometimes pink) up to 2·5cm across; heads borne singly on stems 5—12cm high, opening early in the day but closing at night and in wet weather; each head with short, yellow central florets and spreading, white, petal-like rays; visited by a range of small insects. **Form of plant** clustered rosettes of glossy, spoon-shaped leaves up to 5cm long and lying close to the ground; perennial.
Habitat areas of short grassland — including garden lawns — in lowland and mountainous regions up to 2400m.
Distribution common and abundant throughout Europe.

Ox-eye Daisy

Leucanthemum vulgare

May—September. Large, attractive flowerheads, usually about 4cm across, but sometimes as much as 9cm, borne singly on long stalks; the outer florets of each head are long, forming the conspicuous white rays, the inner florets short and yellow; on the under-side of the flowerhead are three to four rows of purple-edged bracts; attractive to a great variety of insects; fruits are greyish ribbed nutlets.
Form of plant the slightly branched upright flower stems grow 6—100cm high; stem leaves narrow, with large teeth; basal leaves long-stalked, toothed, and spoon-shaped, forming a rosette; very variable; perennial.
Habitat grassland of all kinds including waysides; a weed of gardens and cultivated fields.
Distribution common almost through-out Europe.

Family Liliaceae

Wood Garlic

Allium ursinum

April–June. Attractive star-like flowers with six narrow, pointed petals; each flower, about 1cm across, is grouped with others in a loose, flat-topped cluster (umbel) on a two- or three-angled stem up to 45cm high.
Form of plant the flower stem is associated with a pair of large, bright-green, pointed, oval leaves each with a long, twisted leaf stalk; the whole plant is rather glossy with a strong, nauseating odour of garlic; perennial.
Habitat damp, shady places in woods and thickets, usually in large groups forming a carpet.
Distribution quite common but is sometimes rather localized; grows in most of Europe from Scandinavia and central Russia to Spain, Sicily, and Macedonia.

Lily of the Valley

Convallaria majalis

April–July. Four to twelve pendulous, bell-shaped flowers arranged in a one-sided spike up to 20cm high; each flower is about 8mm across and very fragrant; the fruits are small red berries.
Form of plant the glossy leaves arise as a pair, associated with the flower stem, from an underground stem; each leaf is parallel-veined and oval, with a pointed tip and long stalk, and is 8–20cm long; perennial.
Habitat open woods and thickets with some shade, frequently on limy soils; often cultivated in gardens, from which it sometimes escapes; found at up to 2300m in some mountain regions.
Distribution grows throughout Europe from Scandinavia to northern Spain, Italy, and Greece.

Common Star of Bethlehem

Ornithogalum umbellatum

April—June. Large, pure-white, star-shaped flowers, five to fifteen in a flat-topped cluster; the flowers have six narrow, petal-like segments, each with a broad-green stripe on the back; the cluster is long lived but the flowers open only in sunny weather.

Form of plant small and bulbous with flower stems up to 30cm high; the narrow leaves are rather limp, up to 30cm long and with a white stripe down the midrib; perennial.

Habitat grassy places and scrub, also escaping from gardens and naturalized in waste places; in upland areas found growing up to 1600m.

Distribution widespread in Europe from Mediterranean region northwards to Britain and parts of Scandinavia, but never common.

Common Solomon's Seal

Polygonatum multiflorum

April—June. Arching stems up to 80cm high which bear pendant one-to five-flowered clusters opposite the leaves; the flowers are greenish white and tubular, 9—15mm long, the mouth of the tube with six turned-back lobes; pollinated by bumble-bees; fruits are small, blue-black berries.

Form of plant the green stems grow from an underground stem which is thick, white, and fleshy, with circular scars at intervals giving the plant its common name; the leaves are handsome, pendant, and elliptical, 5—12cm long; perennial.

Habitat woodland and scrub.

Distribution rather rare but found throughout much of Europe from Scandinavia to northern Spain, Italy, and Greece; in Britain, mostly confined to Wales and southern England.

Family Amaryllidaceae

Snowdrop

Galanthus nivalis

January–March. Flowers solitary bell-shaped, and pendulous; each emerges from a delicate, somewhat papery sheath and is borne at the tip of a flower stem up to 25cm high; flowers with three outer pure-white segments about 15mm long surrounding three shorter, green-tipped, notched segments; anthers green; pollinated by bees.

Form of plant two greyish, narrow and angled leaves up to 25cm long; perennial.

Habitat meadows, damp woods and shady stream sides, also widely naturalized as an escape from gardens; in lowland and upland areas up to 2200m.

Distribution not common, sometimes rare, but found throughout much of Europe from Britain and the Netherlands southward to the Pyrenees and westward to Italy, Sicily, and Macedonia.

Family Orchidaceae

Large White Helleborine

Cephalanthera damasonium

May–July. Up to fifteen rather large creamy white flowers in a loose, leafy spike; each flower more or less tubular, unlike the more usual open and spreading orchid flower; the lip is hidden by the outer petals and is blotched and streaked with orange-yellow markings; the ovary beneath the petals is noticeably twisted.

Form of plant the single upright stem grows up to 60cm high with two or three brown scales at the base and several pointed, oval leaves up to 10cm long; perennial.

Habitat in woods and other shady places on chalky soils and particularly in beech woods; in lowland and hilly areas up to 1200m.

Distribution throughout Europe northward to Sweden and eastward to Russia.

Creeping Lady's Tresses

Goodyera repens

July—September. Small, creamy white, highly fragrant flowers in a twisted, one-sided, leafy spike; the lip of each flower is short, pouched, and has the tip turned downwards; spur absent; pollinated by bumble-bees.

Form of plant leafy rosettes with flowering stems 10—25cm high, covered with glandular hairs and bearing dark-green, pointed leaves marked with a network of reddish veins.

Habitat usually among moss in pine-woods, less often under birch trees or on established sand dunes, on acid soils; up to 2200m.

Distribution local and rather rare; grows in northern and central Europe as far south as the Pyrenees and northern Italy; in Britain is restricted to scattered places in north and east England, and in Scotland.

Greater Butterfly Orchid

Platanthera chlorantha

May—August. Dainty, greenish-white or milk-white, long-spurred flowers, 18—23mm across, widely spaced in a cylindrical spike; each flower has a long, twisted ovary bearing two spreading petal segments surmounted by a hood and with a prominent, long, strap-shaped lip below which is striped and blotched with green; usually the flowers are fragrant, especially in the evening, and are attractive to moths.

Form of plant flower stem growing to 60cm high, arising from usually two broadly oval stalked leaves; one to five stem-leaves, which become smaller towards the flowers; perennial.

Habitat meadows, scrub, and woodland, usually on chalky soils and tolerant of deep shade; up to 1800m.

Distribution rather uncommon but found throughout Europe.

Family Ranunculaceae

Stinking Hellebore

Helleborus foetidus

January—May. Branched, drooping clusters of globular yellowish-green flowers; each flower is 1—3cm across, with five purplish-tipped sepals surrounding five to ten green tubular nectaries and numerous stamens; fruits develop usually as three wrinkled pods with black seeds attractive to ants.
Form of plant a branched stem up to 80cm high bears dark-green leaves which overwinter; lower leaves are large and divided into three to nine radiating segments on long, rather reddish stems, upper leaves are small and undivided; all parts with a strong unpleasant odour; perennial.
Habitat dry scrub and woodland on chalky soils also on rock screes; found up to 1800m.
Distribution not common but grows in south-west and central Europe as far north as Britain.

Family Chenopodiaceae

Fat Hen

Chenopodium album

June—October. Minute greenish flowers without petals, densely clustered in branched leafy spikes.
Form of plant very variable especially in leaf shape; the upright, often reddish stems grow 100cm or more high and bear rather fleshy leaves which were formerly eaten as spinach; leaves at the top of the stems are small and slender but towards the base are larger (about 10cm long), toothed and more or less diamond-shaped; all leaves appear white because of a dense mealy covering but if this is scraped off the leaf surface is dark green; annual.
Habitat waste places and cultivated ground, where it can be a very common weed.
Distribution common throughout Europe.

Glasswort

Salicornia europaea

August–September. Extremely inconspicuous flowers in threes between the joints of the upper parts of the stems, the single stamen of each flower somewhat protruding.

Form of plant an unusual little plant with extremely fleshy and translucent, jointed stems and branches; at the junction of each cylindrical joint is a pair of tiny, fleshy leaves; the stems grow 10–35cm high, the whole plant is dark green when young, turning yellowish-green and later becoming flushed with red or purple when the seeds are ripe; very variable; annual.

Habitat muddy salt marshes, where the plants are regularly immersed by sea water; sometimes inland on sandy soils.

Distribution locally abundant, often forming a carpet on the mud; along the coasts of north-west Europe.

Annual Seablite

Suaeda maritima

July–November. Tiny flowers (sometimes red) grouped in one to threes at the base of the upper leaves; flowers without distinct sepals and petals, having five fleshy little segments surrounding five stamens and the ovary.

Form of plant a fleshy, rather untidy herb, usually about 50cm high but sometimes twice as tall; the stems are sprawling or upright, with numerous crowded leaves; leaves are 3–25mm long, pointed, and with a flat upper surface but rounded beneath; young stems and leaves are blue-green in colour but often turn distinctly reddish later; very variable in habit, leaf shape, and colour; annual.

Habitat salt marshes, sandy and muddy seashores, saline areas inland.

Distribution common in much of Europe; not found on Arctic coasts.

Family Rosaceae

Salad Burnet

Sanguisorba minor

May–September. Tiny greenish flowers, sometimes tinged with purple, in small rounded heads 7–12mm across; flowers have four sepals, no petals, and are of three kinds — uppermost flowers female, with tufted crimson stigmas, middle flowers perfect having both stigmas and stamens, lowest flowers male, with thirty to forty long-stalked stamens; wind pollinated.

Form of plant a bluish-green herb smelling of cucumber when crushed, with branched flower stems 60cm or more high; basal leaves in a rosette, with three to twelve pairs of strongly toothed leaflets, stem leaves rather smaller; very variable; perennial.

Habitat dry grassland and rocky ground, especially on chalk or limestone; up to 2200m.

Distribution southern, central, and western Europe; locally common but rare in the south-west.

Family Araliaceae

Ivy

Hedera helix

September–November. Small, yellowish-green, five-petalled flowers in rounded clusters produced on the upper stems but only in sunlight; fruits are small, black berries.

Form of plant an evergreen, woody, climbing or trailing plant with stems up to 25cm across and reaching a height of 30m; masses of small, adhesive roots grow along the stems, attaching themselves to trees, rocks, or walls; other stems may branch and trail along the ground often forming a carpet; leaves dark green (sometimes flushed purple) leathery, and glossy, but differing in shape — those on climbing stems are palmately lobed, on flowering stems they are oval; perennial.

Habitat creeping in woodland or climbing rocks, walls, trees, and hedges.

Distribution common virtually throughout Europe.

Family Euphorbiaceae

Wood Spurge

Euphorbia amygdaloides

March–June. 'Flowers' (bracts and associated structures) borne in umbels of five to ten rays at the top of the stem, with additional rays below; each ray forks into two and these further subdivide; bracts yellowish green and joined at the base in pairs to form an involucre within which are four conspicuous, crescent-shaped glands.

Form of plant a rather stocky, downy herb with one or more reddish, tufted stems up to 90cm high; first-year plants are sterile and the dark-green, spoon-shaped leaves form a terminal rosette; second-year plants produce a stem with pale-green leaves and flowers from the centre of the rosette; perennial.

Habitat damp woods and scrub.

Distribution north-west, central, and southern Europe.

Sun Spurge

Euphorbia helioscopia

April-November. In all spurges the 'flower' is a complex inflorescence in which the bracts are almost like petals and the true flowers very much reduced; in the Sun Spurge the flower stem terminates in a large, five-rayed, spreading umbel with bracts resembling small leaves but more yellowish in colour; within the cup-like involucres are four to five oval green glands.

Form of plant a single usually unbranched stem grows up to 50cm, smooth and slightly reddish with simple leaves up to 3cm long, toothed towards the tip; all parts contain a milky juice (latex); annual.

Habitat waste places and cultivated areas including fields and gardens.

Distribution an extremely common weed of cultivation found throughout Europe.

43

Family Polygonaceae

Black Bindweed

Bilderdykia convolvulus

July—October. Tiny, greenish-pink or greenish-white flowers borne on jointed stalks in small clusters along the stems; fruits dull black and slightly rough, about 4mm across, with three narrow, whitish wings.

Form of plant a scrambling or twining herb with stems up to 100cm long bearing large, widely spaced arrow- to heart-shaped leaves; without the flowers it could be mistaken for a true bindweed but can be distinguished by its stems twisting clockwise and by the white, mealy surface of its stems and undersides of its leaves; annual.

Habitat waste places and cultivated land such as fields and gardens, formerly a troublesome weed in corn-fields.

Distribution common throughout Europe except in arctic regions.

Common Sorrel

Rumex acetosa

May—August. Tiny, greenish flowers becoming red with age; male and female flowers on separate plants, in dense whorled spikes at the ends of the stem and branches; flowers, lacking obvious sepals and petals, have six small segments arranged in two whorls of three; wind pollinated.

Form of plant a slender herb which may reach 100cm, often less; basal leaves long stalked and arrow-shaped, grow in a rosette with the lobes at the base pointing downwards; stem leaves without stalks and clasping the stems; a delicate fringed sheath (ochrea) surrounds the stem just above each leaf base; very variable; perennial.

Habitat open woodland and grassland; up to 2300m.

Distribution widespread and common in most of Europe; rare in the south.

Family Urticaceae

Stinging Nettle

Urtica dioica

June—September. Tiny greenish flowers in branched, pendant, catkin-like clusters up to 10cm long; male and female flowers on separate plants; wind pollinated.

Form of plant a well-known, coarse-looking plant with erect leafy stems usually up to 150cm high, but particularly robust specimens can reach 250cm; leaves in pairs, 4—8cm long, pointed and heart-shaped with strongly toothed margins; stems and leaves covered with stinging hairs which break when touched, injecting an irritant fluid into the skin; perennial.

Habitat woodlands, hedgebanks, fens, grassy and waste places, often near buildings and on rubble and litter; in lowland and upland areas up to 3125m.

Distribution common throughout Europe and temperate parts of the whole world.

Family Cannabaceae

Hemp

Cannabis sativa

June—September. Tiny greenish flowers somewhat tinged with pink, either male or female and growing on separate plants; male flowers stalked, each with five stamens surrounded by five green segments, borne in much-branched open clusters; female flowers not stalked, growing in spikes; wind pollinated; fruits are small nutlets.

Form of plant a strong-smelling, upright herb with leafy stems up to 2·5m high; leaves large and fan-shaped, deeply divided into three to nine narrow toothed lobes; annual.

Habitat waste, often sandy ground, but also widely grown on the Continent for its fibre, oil, and narcotic resin.

Distribution except where cultivated it is rather rare; a native plant of south-east Russia but now found in many other parts of Europe.

Hop

Humulus lupulus

July–September. Rather inconspicuous male and female flowers on separate plants, both are grouped into widely differing flowerheads; male heads are much branched and feathery; female heads resemble small green 'cones' and are of economic importance because they are used to flavour beer; the female heads consist of a number of yellowish-green, somewhat papery bracts which hide the flowers, later the heads enlarge becoming about 5cm long when ripe.

Form of plant a herbaceous climber with stems up to 6m tall which twist clockwise; the roughly hairy leaves are large and ornamental, palmately divided into about five deeply cut lobes; perennial.

Habitat hedges and scrub, also widely cultivated.

Distribution widely found (although not common) in most of Europe.

Family Plantaginaceae

Great Plantain

Plantago major

May–October. Long, cylindrical, greenish spikes, 10–50cm long, with numerous, tiny, tightly packed flowers; individual flowers about 3mm across, with a minute, yellowish, four-lobed corolla and four long-stalked, purple stamens, which later turn yellowish brown; pollinated by wind; fruits are small capsules each opening by a circular lid.

Form of plant a rosette of large, broadly oval leaves, 15cm or more in length, long stalked and with three to nine conspicuous, parallel veins, the flower stems arising from the centre of the rosette; perennial.

Habitat waysides, meadows, fields, gardens, paths, and waste places; often a troublesome weed, especially in lawns; up to 2800m.

Distribution very common throughout Europe and naturalized in many other parts of the world.

Family Adoxaceae

Townhall Clock

Adoxa moschatellina

March-June. Flowers minute, grouped in fives in tight little heads at the tips of the stems; four of the flowers face outwards (like a townhall clock or the four points of the compass) with the fifth on top and facing upwards.

Form of plant stems 5—15cm high with a few long-stalked leaves which are subdivided into threes; the whole plant is smooth, light-green in colour, and has a faint musky scent; perennial.

Habitat in woods, hedgerows, and other shady places; often forms a dense carpet; also among rocks on mountain slopes up to 2370m.

Distribution not uncommon throughout Europe from Scandinavia to central Spain and eastwards to Italy and Bulgaria.

Family Orchidaceae

Common Twayblade

Listera ovata

May—July. A long, rather open spike of small, yellowish-green flowers, each with a narrow, deeply forked lip 10—15mm long and borne on a more-or-less globular ovary.

Form of plant as its common name suggests, this orchid has only two leaves (in an opposite pair) each up to 20cm long, roughly oval in shape with three to five prominent parallel veins; between them arises the flower stem 20—60cm high; perennial.

Habitat tolerating moisture and dryness, acid and alkaline soils, sunshine and shade; found in meadows and woods, sometimes on sand dunes; in lowland and mountain areas up to 2300m.

Distribution common throughout Europe, even north of the Arctic Circle; rare in Mediterranean regions.

Family Papaveraceae

Field Poppy

Papaver rhoeas

May—October. Large, solitary, scarlet (rarely pink or white) flowers, the four delicate crumpled petals often blotched with black at the base; buds drooping, with two hairy sepals which soon fall; within are numerous purplish-black stamens and a rounded, flat-topped ovary with eight to twelve radiating stigmas; visited by insects for pollen.

Form of plant upright, branched stems up to 90cm high; leaves toothed and pinnately lobed, the terminal lobe large with the other lobes pointing towards it; stems and leaves rough with spreading bristles and exuding a poisonous, milky juice if damaged; annual.

Habitat waste places, disturbed ground, and, less commonly, cultivated fields; up to 1750m.

Distribution common throughout Europe except the far north.

Family Caryophyllaceae

Red Campion

Silene dioica

May—September. Unscented rose-red (rarely white) flowers, 18—25mm across, in forked clusters; flowers either male or female, on separate plants; each flower has five deeply cleft petals and five pairs of narrow scales at the throat of the tube; the five-toothed calyx is egg-shaped in female flowers, cylindrical in male flowers; visited by bumble-bees and hover-flies.

Form of plant a hairy, almost sticky herb with erect flowering stems up to 90cm tall and shorter, spreading, non-flowering stems; leaves paired, oval, and pointed; biennial or perennial.

Habitat moist places in hedgerows, woods, and clearings, also on sea cliffs, rocks, and scree slopes; up to 2360m.

Distribution widespread in Europe, rare in some areas, abundant in others.

Family Primulaceae

Scarlet Pimpernel

Anagallis arvensis

May—October. Star-like flowers (sometimes pink, blue, white or lilac) opening only in fine weather and borne on long thin stalks in pairs along the stems; petals have hairy edges and fine teeth at the tips; pink or white flowers have a red eye; the small, spherical fruits open by a dome-shaped lid.

Form of plant sprawling, branched stems grow 6–30cm long and bear small, simple, paired leaves; stems and the undersides of the leaves are dotted with tiny black glands; annual.

Habitat cultivated areas such as fields and gardens, also by roadsides and on sand dunes.

Distribution common throughout Europe — is, in fact, found in most parts of the world except the tropics.

Family Valerianaceae

Red Valerian

Centranthus ruber

May—September. Small, sweet-scented flowers (sometimes pink or white) in much-branched, rounded clusters at the ends of stems and branches; flowers slender and tubular, about 10mm long, with a long, nectar-containing spur, visited by long-tongued insects especially butterflies and moths; the small fruits are crowned with a tiny, hairy parachute and are blown away by the wind.

Form of plant a handsome, upright herb (woody at the base) up to 80cm high with large, undivided, pointed, oval leaves; both stems and leaves are smooth and distinctly grey-green in colour; perennial.

Habitat waste places, railway banks, old walls, chalk pits, limestone quarries, rocks, and cliffs.

Distribution common throughout central and southern Europe; naturalized as a garden escape in Britain.

Family Compositae

Mugwort

Artemisia vulgaris

July–September. Florets tiny and brownish-red in colour (sometimes yellowish), borne in many small flower-heads each not more than 4mm across; the heads are surrounded by white, woolly bracts and are grouped into much-branched inflorescences; the florets are wind pollinated.

Form of plant a rather bushy herb with hairy, reddish stems up to 120cm high; the leaves are markedly pinnately lobed and toothed, dark green above but white with a dense coating of hairs beneath; all parts are slightly aromatic; individual plants show great variability in leaf form and the amount of branching in the inflorescences; perennial.

Habitat waysides, hedgerows, and waste places.

Distribution common throughout Europe except in the extreme south.

Family Papaveraceae

Common Fumitory

Fumaria officinalis

April–October. Small, irregular, four-petalled flowers, the uppermost petal with a nectar-filled spur at its base, in dense spikes of at least twenty flowers; petals purplish-pink, usually tipped with purple or dark red.

Form of plant a rather variable, bluish-green, spreading or climbing herb with flower stems 30–90cm high; the long slender pinnately subdivided leaves have twisting leaf stalks which enable the plant to climb other plants; the leaves form a tuft at the base of the plant and are also borne along the stems; annual.

Habitat dry waste places and cultivated ground, especially in lighter soils.

Distribution virtually throughout Europe except the extreme north; a common plant in eastern Europe, somewhat less so towards the west.

Family Caryophyllaceae

Maiden Pink

Dianthus deltoides

June—September. Flowers 18mm across (sometimes white), either solitary or less commonly in twos or threes, at the tips of the main stem and branches; petals rose-pink, spotted white, with a crimson ring at the throat, and toothed edges; the flowers close in dull weather; visited by butterflies and moths.

Form of plant a much-branched herb forming a loose mat of creeping and upright flowering stems, dull blue-green and leafy; leaves narrow and, like the stems, roughly hairy; perennial.

Habitat dry sandy or gravelly banks, fields and other grassy places, also hilly pastures.

Distribution a rather rare plant found throughout Europe as far north as Norway, Finland, and northern Russia.

Ragged Robin

Lychnis flos-cuculi

May—August. Untidy looking, rose-coloured flowers (rarely white) in open, forked clusters; each flower is 3—4cm across with five petals, each deeply cut into four narrow lobes, the inner lobes very long, encircled by a reddish, five-toothed calyx striped with ten conspicuous veins; visited by butterflies and bees for nectar; the fruit is a capsule opening by five small teeth, enclosed by the persistent calyx.

Form of plant erect flowering stems up to 90cm high, and spreading non-flowering stems; leaves pointed, oval, up to 10cm long; stems and leaves are rough, the upper stems rather sticky; perennial.

Habitat marshy places, damp meadows and woods; up to 2500m.

Distribution common throughout most of Europe, rare in the south.

Family Geraniaceae

Soapwort

Herb Robert

Saponaria officinalis

Geranium robertianum

June—October. Attractive, scented, pale-pink (sometimes white) five-petalled flowers (sometimes double) in rather dense, forked clusters; each flower about 2·5cm across; the base of the petals surrounded by five joined sepals, each petal with two tiny scales at the throat of the flower; visited chiefly by hawkmoths (day and night).
Form of plant a robust herb with creeping stems and upright flower stems which may reach 90cm; all stems leafy, the leaves smooth, dark green, pointed, and oval; perennial.
Habitat hedgebanks, roadsides, and waste ground, often near dwelling-places and probably an escape from cultivation; sometimes by streams and in damp woodland.
Distribution fairly common in much of Europe northwards to Britain, Belgium, and Germany.

April—November. Bright pink flowers (occasionally white) 10—15mm across, the five petals strongly veined; flowers in pairs hang downwards at night and in bad weather; fruits wrinkled and hairy, splitting into single-seeded segments from which the seeds are ejected.
Form of plant a branched rather sprawling herb 10—50cm high, bright green but with a reddish tinge which becomes much more pronounced towards the autumn; stems reddish, rather succulent yet fragile, and hairy; the leaves long stalked and palmately cut into three to five deeply lobed leaflets; stems and leaves emit a pungent odour; annual or biennial.
Habitat woods, hedgebanks, walls, stony places, among rocks and on shingle; found up to 2000m.
Distribution common throughout Europe except the extreme north.

Family Papilionaceae

Rest-harrow

Ononis repens

June—September. Attractive little rose-pink, pea-like flowers (sometimes purple) growing singly or paired, at intervals along the leafy stems; each flower has a prominent often reddish-veined standard at the back and is visited by bees for pollen; the fruits are short, few-seeded pods hidden within the joined sepals.

Form of plant a much-branched spreading or upright shrubby little plant 30—70cm high, the stems often rooting where they touch the ground; the stems bear silvery, rather sticky leaves with stipules and either one or three toothed leaflets, and may end in soft spines; rather variable; perennial.

Habitat rough grassland, poorly culti-vated fields and barren sandy places near the sea.

Distribution common in western and ntral Europe.

Family Rosaceae

Dog Rose

Rosa canina

June—July. Large attractive and well-known flowers, borne singly or up to five together, scented or unscented, varying in colour from blush-pink to white; the five broad petals surround numerous stamens and styles and are borne on top of the swollen ovary which will, after pollination, become the familiar scarlet rose-hip; visited by various insects for the abundant pollen.

Form of plant a robust shrub often forming a bush with branched arching stems 1—3m high bearing many stout, hooked prickles; leaves pinnately divided into five to seven dark-green toothed leaflets; very variable, the species often subdivided; perennial.

Habitat scrub, hedgerows, woodland and grassy places; up to 2200m.

Distribution common throughout Europe.

Family Polygonaceae

Common Knotgrass

Polygonum aviculare

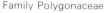

June—November. Tiny, star-shaped flowers (pink or white) in clusters of one to six in the angle between stem and leaf, surrounded overall by a delicate silvery sheath (ochrea); each flower with five minute, petal-like segments, flesh-pink or greenish-white; fruits are tiny, three-angled brown nutlets.

Form of plant a slender, sprawling herb with stems 3—200cm long; leaves rather widely spaced, narrow, pointed, up to 5cm long; an extremely variable species; annual.

Habitat waste ground, roadsides, fields and gardens — often a very common weed — also by the seashore; reaching 2300m, with a dwarf alpine variety found as high as 2700m.

Distribution extremely common and and cosmopolitan, being found in all parts of the world except the polar regions.

Family Ericaceae

Bog Rosemary

Andromeda polifolia

May—September. Long-stalked, flesh-pink flowers (sometimes white) in clusters of two to eight at the ends of the leafy stems; each flower is more or less globular, 6—7mm across, and drooping; pollination is by bumble-bees and butterflies both of which have tongues long enough to reach the nectar.

Form of plant a low-growing, ever-green shrub with sparingly branched stems up to 40cm high; the leaves are small, narrow, and pointed, with in-rolled margins, glossy green above and whitish below; perennial.

Habitat peat bogs and wet heaths in upland areas, and may be found at up to 2000m on some mountains.

Distribution a rather rare plant of northern Europe, also the Alps and Pyrenees.

Family Pyrolaceae

Common Wintergreen

Pyrola minor

May–September. Unusual little pinkish flowers (sometimes white), about 6mm across, nearly spherical in shape; all parts in fives, the mouth of the flower almost plugged by the stamens and large, five-lobed stigma; flowers rather densely arranged on a long-stalked leafless stem 5–30cm high.

Form of plant a low-growing herb with a cluster of stalked, oval, light-green leaves up to 7cm long; perennial.

Habitat moors, scrub, woods, marshes, preferring humus-rich soils but also on established sand dunes and wet rock ledges; in lowland and mountain areas up to 2700m.

Distribution not common but grows throughout much of Europe, becoming rarer in the south; absent from most of Wales, the Channel Islands, Isle of Man, and parts of Scotland.

Family Plumbaginaceae

Thrift

Armeria maritima

March–October. Flowers pale to deep rose-pink (sometimes white), small, fragrant, and rather papery, with parts in fives; the flowers are clustered in roundish heads about 2cm across, borne singly on downy leafless stems up to 20cm high; just beneath each flowerhead are brownish papery bracts, some of them sheathing the top of the stem; the central flower is always the first to open.

Form of plant dense cushiony tufts of fleshy, rather grass-like leaves but varying considerably in size and leaf form; perennial.

Habitat coastal rocks and cliff tops, muddy or sandy soils near the coast, less commonly in stony mountain meadows up to 2900m.

Distribution common throughout most of Europe except the south-east.

Family Primulaceae

Common Cyclamen

Cyclamen purpurascens

June—October. Carmine-pink, sweetly scented flowers about 1·5cm across, of a characteristic and unusual shape with the five pointed petals turned back on themselves, each flower borne singly on a long, bare stalk; when in fruit these stalks curl round like a watch-spring carrying the fruits down to the ground.

Form of plant a low-growing herb (barely 15cm) with flower stalks and leaves arising from a fleshy, flattened corm; leaves leathery, rounded to heart-shaped, dark green above with silvery blotches, reddish-purple beneath; perennial.

Habitat shady woodland or scrub, often on stony soil especially limestone; not so common as its name suggests.

Distribution central and south-east Europe, usually in upland areas, reaching 1800m in the Alps.

Sea Milkwort

Glaux maritima

May—September. Small bell-shaped flowers (sometimes white or purple) without petals but with five coloured sepals alternating with five stamens; flowers solitary in the axils of the upper leaves.

Form of plant a small, fleshy plant not more than 30cm high, with creeping rooting stems and opposite pairs of small, simple, bluish-green leaves; perennial.

Habitat in grassy salt marshes and on seashores among rocks and at the foot of cliffs, also on saline soils inland; often forming thick patches.

Distribution localized but fairly common along the Arctic, Baltic, and Atlantic coasts of Europe; rather rare in the western Mediterranean region; found inland in Spain, central and eastern Europe.

Family Convolvulaceae

Lesser Bindweed

Convolvulus arvensis

May—October. Handsome, broadly funnel-shaped flowers (also pink and white, or white) up to 3cm across; slightly fragrant, opening only in sunny weather but soon withering; borne either singly or in twos or threes at intervals along the stem.

Form of plant a trailing or climbing herb with slender stems that twist anti-clockwise around other plants, growing to 75cm long; leaves stalked, more or less arrow-shaped, 2·5cm long; perennial.

Habitat waste and grassy places, beside roads and railways, sometimes in short turf near the sea but probably best known as a serious weed of cultivated land, especially light soils; in lowland and upland areas to 2000m.

Distribution common throughout Europe.

Family Scrophulariaceae

Lesser Snapdragon

Misopates orontium

June—October. Small purplish-pink flowers (rarely white) widely spaced in a leafy spike; each flower is two-lipped and pouched, with a yellow throat, and has the appearance of a small garden Antirrhinum; around the base of each flower are five, long, spreading sepal lobes; pollinated by bees.

Form of plant a slender, narrow-leaved herb, sparingly branched and hairy, with stems up to 50cm high; annual.

Habitat usually on cultivated land, where it may be found as a rather rare weed, also on bare sandy places.

Distribution essentially a plant of southern, western, and central Europe but spreading as a weed northwards and eastwards, never in the far north.

Red Bartsia

Odontites verna

June—October. Leafy spikes of reddish-pink or purplish-pink flowers (rarely white) which all face the same way, each two-lipped, the lower lip larger and three-lobed, and with a long, projecting, purplish stigma; pollinated by bees which visit the flowers for nectar.

Form of plant a rather purplish downy plant with branched leafy stems up to 50cm high, semiparasitic on the roots of grasses; leaves lance-shaped with toothed margins; very variable in form and time of flowering; annual.

Habitat waste ground, roadsides, grassland, and cultivated fields; in lowland and upland areas up to 1800m.

Distribution common in most of Europe but absent from some islands such as Crete, Greece, and Iceland.

Common Lousewort

Pedicularis sylvatica

April—July. Strongly two-lipped, rose-pink flowers (sometimes red, rarely white) 2—2·5cm long in terminal leafy spikes; upper lip of each flower hooded (with two teeth near the tip), the lower lip with three rounded lobes; sepals forming a brownish tube ending in five unequal teeth, one strap-shaped and the other four pointed, and with green, leafy tips.

Form of plant an upright stem 5—25cm high with a number of sprawling branches from the base; all stems leafy and often purplish, the leaves pinnately dissected so that they appear feathery; perennial or biennial.

Habitat bogs, damp heaths, and grassland also damp woods, usually on peaty soils; up to 1700m.

Distribution common throughout western and central Europe.

Family Labiatae
Common Hemp-nettle
Galeopsis tetrahit

July—October. Distinctly two-lipped flowers (sometimes purple, yellow, or white) up to 20mm across, in leafy whorls at the ends of the flower stems; the upper lip hooded and somewhat hairy, the lower three-lobed, marbled with darker markings; lips joined at the base to form a tube hidden within a bristly five-toothed calyx.

Form of plant a branched herb with rough-haired stems 10—100cm high bearing pairs of pointed, oval, toothed leaves; characteristically the stems are swollen beneath each leafy pair, each swelling bearing red-tipped, glandular hairs; annual.

Habitat open situations — roadsides, hedgerows, cultivated fields, woodland clearings, heaths, and fens; in lowland and upland areas to 2660m.

Distribution common in most of Europe, becoming rare in the south-east.

Family Orchidaceae
Common Spotted Orchid
Dactylorhiza fuchsii

May—August. Dense, pointed spikes of attractive flowers which vary in colour from deep lilac-pink to white; each flower is about 1cm across, with a straight spur and a conspicuous three-lobed lip variably streaked and spotted with reddish markings.

Form of plant the flower stems grow 50cm or more high and bear five to twenty lance-shaped leaves blotched pale or dark purple but sometimes unspotted; very variable in number, shape, and spotting of the leaves; perennial.

Habitat meadows, woods, and scrub, in wet and dry places on both limy and sandy acid soils; up to 1825m.

Distribution the commonest orchid in northern and central Europe; sometimes divided into two or more species.

59

Family Ranunculaceae

Fragrant Orchid

Gymnadenia conopsea

May–August. Small somewhat purplish-pink flowers (sometimes white or magenta-red) with long, slender, nectar-containing spurs, and in a dense spike usually 6–10cm long; the flowers have a strong almost sickly scent (sometimes of cloves) although some specimens may be odourless; each flower has rather spreading lateral segments and a lip with three rounded lobes; pollination is by moths.

Form of plant the flower stem is 15–40cm high, slightly purple, and with up to eight rather long and narrow, unspotted leaves; perennial.

Habitat open woods, fens, marshes, fields, and grassy slopes usually on chalk or limestone, occasionally on acid heaths; up to 2450m.

Distribution fairly common but generally localized in regions throughout Europe.

Columbine

Aquilegia vulgaris

May–July. Attractive pendant flowers (sometimes blue, pink, or white) of an unusual shape, with each of the five petals prolonged into a nectar-secreting horn-shaped spur; both sepals and petals coloured; flowers visited by long-tongued bumble-bees for pollen and nectar; fruits a cluster of five rather papery pods which begin to open while still green.

Form of plant a herb with leafy flower stems up to 100cm high; leaves smooth, folded into pleats when in bud, much divided into lobed leaflets; perennial.

Habitat moist, usually limy, soils in open woods and scrub in lowland and hilly areas.

Distribution an uncommon plant mainly of southern and central Europe but growing as far north as Britain and southern Sweden.

Pasque Flower

Pulsatilla vulgaris

March—May. Large, solitary flowers which droop slightly on their stalks; each flower is bell-shaped, with six dull, violet sepals taking the place of petals, and is surrounded by a frill of finely divided bracts; there are numerous stamens, the outer ones being transformed into nectaries; at the centre are ·many young fruits which later become a cluster of plumed nutlets; flowers much visited by bees for both pollen and nectar.

Form of plant a rosette of feathery basal leaves surrounds the flower stems; all parts of the plant, including the outside of the flowers, are densely covered with long, silky hairs; perennial.

Habitat dry chalky pastures and hill slopes.

Distribution in central and northern Europe; not common.

Purple Corydalis

Corydalis solida

March—May. Irregular, dull-purple, four-petalled flowers (sometimes whitish), each about 20mm in length, with a long, straight spur on the upper petal; ten to twenty flowers are borne in a terminal spike, each flower associated with a deeply lobed bract; long-tongued bees visit for nectar within the spurs.

Form of plant a rather delicate, bluish-green herb about 20cm high; the single, unbranched flower stem bears one· to three much-divided leaves, the leaflet in threes, with a short, strap-shaped bract below; perennial.

Habitat shady hedgerows and woods (also orchards); in upland areas up to 2000m.

Distribution fairly common in most of Europe except the extreme north and west; rare in the Mediterranean region; in Britain only where escaped from gardens.

Family Cruciferae

Sea Rocket

Cakile maritima

June—September. Sweet-scented, four-petalled flowers (sometimes pink or white) about 2cm across which are borne in dense spikes at the ends of the branches; the flowers show a wide colour range and are attractive to bees, flies, and other insects; the fruits are unusual, consisting of two single-seeded joints which separate and are carried away by tides.

Form of plant bushy, with zigzag, branched, erect, and also prostrate stems reaching 45cm long; the leaves are up to 6cm long, undivided or pinnately lobed, smooth, greyish, and fleshy; annual.

Habitat coastal sand and shingle, close to the high-water mark, and on salt marshes.

Distribution common along both northern and southern coasts of Europe.

Cuckoo Flower

Cardamine pratensis

April—July. Attractive spikes of up to twenty lilac-purple flowers (occasionally pale pink or white); each flower about 15mm across and with the four-petalled structure characteristic of its family; the ripe fruits are pods which open explosively, splitting into two coils and ejecting the seeds for distances of up to 2m.

Form of plant a rather variable, medium-sized herb with smooth, leafy flowering stems arising from a basal rosette; all leaves are pinnate and slightly hairy but stem leaves have much narrower leaflets than basal leaves; perennial.

Habitat damp meadows and woods, stream-sides, and other wet grassy places in both lowland and upland areas.

Distribution common throughout Europe and may be found at altitudes of up to 2600m.

Honesty

Lunaria annua

April–June. Reddish-purple, white, or striped, unscented flowers in an open, branched or unbranched spike; each flower about 3cm across, with four, broad petals forming a cross; insect visitors include butterflies and long-tongued bees; fruits very distinctive, flat, almost circular and about 25mm across; when ripe, the fruit splits to reveal a silvery septum and winged seeds.

Form of plant in the first year a dense rosette of large, toothed, heart-shaped leaves develops; in the second year a stout, leafy flower stem grows up to 100cm high; biennial.

Habitat thickets, hedgerows, and waste places, really a garden escape.

Distribution a native of south-east Europe but naturalized in many other parts of Europe.

Family Violaceae

Sweet Violet

Viola odorata

February–May, August–September. Deep-purple, sweet-scented flowers (also white, rarely pink, or apricot) single on slender, arching stalks up to 15cm high; each flower about 15mm across, with an irregular corolla of five petals; the largest spurred, lateral petals smaller, each with a central hairy line; two of the five green sepals also spurred; later small, green non-opening flowers set seed.

Form of plant a small herb with a tuft of long-stalked, heart-shaped leaves and several long runners rooting at the tips; the leaves produced in mid-summer are larger; perennial.

Habitat hedge-banks, scrub, less often woodland, usually on chalky soils.

Distribution quite common in most of Europe except the far north and south.

Wild Pansy

Viola tricolor

April—November. Attractive, five-petalled flowers, about 2·5cm across, varying in colour from all yellow to purple with a yellow-blotched throat, also bicoloured flowers having some petals purple and some yellow; longest petal with a long, curved spur; pollinated chiefly by long-tongued bees.
Form of plant much-branched, sprawling, angular stems usually not more than 45cm long; leaves very variable in shape, oval to oblong, with a pair of large, leafy and lobed stipules; annual to perennial.
Habitat cultivated fields, waste and grassy places, established sand dunes, not usually on limy soils; up to 2700m.
Distribution found throughout most of Europe, often common but sometimes localized; confined to mountains in the extreme south.

Family Caryophyllaceae

Corn Cockle

Agrostemma githago

May—August. Handsome, red-purple flowers with five large petals which alternate with the long, conspicuous, and spreading teeth of the sepals; the flowers are borne singly at the ends of the branches and, although lacking scent, are much visited by ·butterflies; later the dry fruits develop large, black seeds.
Form of plant an upright herb with a single, slightly branched flowering stem up to 100cm high; leaves narrowly oval, up to 12cm long; all parts covered with long, silky, closely pressed hairs; annual.
Habitat cornfields.
Distribution essentially a weed of cornfields and almost certainly introduced into many European countries from its original home in the Mediterranean region. Now uncommon because of modern methods of çleaning grain.

Family Malvaceae

Common Mallow

Malva sylvestris

May—October. Showy rose-purple flowers 25—40mm across, with five purple-veined, heart-shaped petals spirally twisted in the bud; when first open there is a central column of many stamens, which droop after their pollen is shed exposing numerous styles then ready for pollination; fruits are a circle of single-seeded segments within the calyx, in appearance rather like a small, round cheese.

Form of plant in early summer rather handsome but later becoming ragged; 45—150cm high, with dark-green, palmately lobed basal leaves; stem leaves more deeply lobed; very variable in habit; perennial.

Habitat waste ground, roadsides, meadows, and copses; up to 1820m.

Distribution common throughout most of Europe, becoming scarce in the far north.

Family Geraniaceae

Common Storksbill

Erodium cicutarium

April—September. Rose-purple flowers 1cm across in radiating clusters of three to seven; flowers five-petalled, the upper two petals sometimes blotched at the base; petals often dropping early; the fruit is a cluster of five single-seeded nutlets surmounted by a beak-like structure 2—4cm long; when ripe the beak becomes spirally twisted splitting into five sections which spring apart, each carrying a seed with it.

Form of plant very variable, tufted, and up to 60cm high, with hairy, often sticky stems; leaves pinnately subdivided; annual.

Habitat dry fields, meadows, and waste places mainly on sandy soils, also on dunes.

Distribution common in coastal areas, less common inland; up to 2100m in mountain areas; found throughout Europe.

Family Papilionaceae

Lucerne

Medicago sativa

May—September. Five to forty pea-like flowers crowded together in long-stalked spikes towards the ends of the stems; although commonly purplish or sometimes yellow, hybrids may be green or almost black; this and related species have characteristic spirally coiled, pod-like fruits.

Form of plant an upright, softly hairy herb with leafy stems up to 90cm high; the leaves have three leaflets, rather like a clover leaf, but toothed at the tips and with a pair of slender stipules at the base; extremely variable in shape of fruits as well as flower colour; perennial.

Habitat waste, grassy, and cultivated areas; grown as a fodder plant, frequently escaping.

Distribution originally in the Mediterranean region, now widespread in most of Europe except the north.

Red Clover

Trifolium pratense

May—October. Terminal, rounded heads of small, sweet-scented reddish-purple or pinkish-purple flowers (rarely cream or white), the heads about 30mm across, single or paired, with two trifoliate leaves close to the base; flowers pea-shaped, visited by bees for nectar.

Form of plant an upright or spreading herb with branched stems 5—100cm high; leaves stalked and trifoliate, the three leaflets elliptical and often marked with a curved, whitish band; at the base of the leaf stalk is a pair of long-pointed stipules; extremely variable; perennial.

Habitat pastures, waste and grassy places on well-drained, fertile soils, often cultivated as a hay crop; up to 3150m.

Distribution common throughout Europe except for the extreme north and south.

Tufted Vetch

Vicia cracca

June–August. Blue-purple pea-like flowers crowded in one-sided spikes 2–10cm long; each flower is drooping, short stalked, and 8–12mm across; pollinated by bees which visit for nectar; fruit a pod 10–25mm long.

Form of plant a climbing herb with weak stems reaching to 200cm, which scramble among other plants by means of tendrils; long leaves, each with six to fifteen pairs of narrow leaflets and a terminal, branched tendril; at the base of each leaf is a pair of stipules, each half-arrow-shaped; perennial.

Habitat hedgerows, woodland edges and clearings, fields, and other grassy places; up to 2230m.

Distribution common and widely distributed throughout Europe.

Common Vetch

Vicia sativa

April–September. Dainty, short stalked flowers, single or paired, at the base of the leaves; flower colour rather variable, some being bicoloured purple and blue; each flower 10–30mm across, producing nectar which is attractive to bees; fruit a slender pod up to 8cm long.

Form of plant a downy, trailing or climbing herb with stems reaching 120cm long, and pinnate leaves; each leaf has stipules half-arrow-shaped often with a dark blotch, and three to eight pairs of leaflets, each having a fine, hair-like tip; very variable in size and shape of leaves and flowers; annual.

Habitat hedgerows, roadsides, fields, waste, and grassy places, often cultivated for fodder; up to 2400m.

Distribution common throughout Europe.

Family Rosaceae

Marsh Cinquefoil

Potentilla palustris

May–August. Somewhat dingy flowers in loose clusters at the tips of the stems; all flower parts deep- or reddish-purple; the five petals alternate with five broad sepals (which are twice the length of the petals) and surround the numerous stamens; outside the sepals is an epicalyx of five slender teeth; the fruits are collections of small nutlets.

Form of plant upright leafy stems growing to 45cm; the slightly reddish leaves are pinnate with three to seven toothed leaflets, and have long, rather membranous stipules; perennial.

Habitat bogs and marshes, wet heaths and meadows, generally on acid soils; growing to 2100m in upland areas.

Distribution throughout much of Europe from the far north to Spain, Italy, and Bulgaria.

Family Lythraceae

Purple Loosestrife

Lythrum salicaria

June–September. Handsome, tapering spikes of bright rosy purple flowers but, despite the name, the plant is not related to Yellow Loosestrife; the six-petalled flowers are in dense leafy whorls, each flower 10–15mm across; although the flowers from different plants look alike, there are actually three distinct types with short, medium, or long styles, three sizes of pollen grains, and differing lengths of stamen; such devices aid cross-pollination.

Form of plant erect sparingly branched angular stems grow 50–150cm high and bear, long, narrow leaves, heart-shaped at the base, in pairs or threes; perennial.

Habitat fens, marshes, lake sides, and river banks, usually among reeds, often in large clumps.

Distribution locally abundant, found almost throughout Europe except the far north.

Family Onagraceae

Rosebay Willowherb

Epilobium angustifolium

June–September. Attractive flowers held horizontally in long, dense spikes; each flower 2–3cm across, with four slender, purplish sepals alternating with four rose-purple petals; pod-like fruits up to 8cm long splitting when ripe to release numerous plumed seeds which are wind dispersed.
Form of plant an erect, rather striking herb with flowering stems up to 150cm or more high; leaves densely and spirally arranged along the stem, each long and lance-shaped with wavy edges; variable in habit; perennial.
Habitat an adaptable plant found in many situations including cleared and burnt woodland, bomb-sites, waste places, disturbed ground, rocky places, and screes; up to 2530m.
Distribution increasingly common throughout Europe except in the south; formerly rare.

Great Hairy Willowherb

Epilobium hirsutum

July–August. Pinkish-purple flowers, 15–23mm across, in open, leafy spikes at the ends of the stem and branches; flowers with four, broad, notched petals, the four sepals pointed and green; fruits downy and pod-like with numerous brownish-red, plumed seeds.
Form of plant a stout, very hairy, branched herb up to 200cm high; leaves 6–12cm long, lance-shaped with sharply toothed margins, upper leaves shorter than lower; all leaves in pairs, with leaf bases half-clasping the stems; hairiness of stems and leaves very variable; perennial.
Habitat ditches, stream banks, marshes, fens, and other damp places.
Distribution common throughout Europe as far north as southern Sweden.

Family Ericaceae

Heather

Calluna vulgaris

July–October. Leafy spikes of small, long-lasting, bell-shaped flowers (sometimes white) with petals hidden by rose-purple sepals; insects, especially bees, visit the flowers for nectar.

Form of plant a bushy, much-branched shrub about 50cm high, sometimes reaching 100cm; the tiny, evergreen, often hairy leaves grow close together in four rows along the stems; perennial.

Habitat heath, moorland, and boggy areas also in open woods, always on acid soils; sometimes on sandy soils near the sea.

Distribution common and often growing in dense masses over wide areas; in lowland and upland regions up to 2720m; found throughout Europe from Finland southwards to Spain and eastwards to Greece; much more common in western Europe.

Bell Heather

Erica cinerea

May–September. Small, reddish-purple, bell-shaped flowers in irregular, whorled, leafy clusters at the ends of the branches; much visited by bumble-bees for nectar.

Form of plant a spreading, evergreen shrub, up to 75cm high, with branched, wiry stems rooting at the base; the tiny, smooth, needle-like leaves are dark green, often with a bronze flush; the leaves grow in threes, together with short, leafy shoots which look like tufts of leaves; perennial.

Habitat drier parts of heaths and moors, open woods, rocky ground; strictly confined to acid soils; in upland areas to 1550m.

Distribution western Europe from Norway to northern Spain and Portugal and eastwards to north-west Italy.

Family Plumbaginaceae

Sea Lavender

Limonium vulgare

July—October. Small, five-petalled, un-scented, bluish-purple flowers, many together in small spikes grouped into one-sided, branched, flat-topped clusters about 10cm across; visited for nectar by bees, beetles, and flies.

Form of plant smooth, leafless flower stems grow from a stout, woody base, each stem up to 70cm high; the leaves grow in a basal rosette and are hairless, variable in shape, but usually roughly oblong ending in a fine, hair-like point; leaf size varies from 10—15cm long and 15—40mm wide; perennial.

Habitat muddy seacoasts and estuarine salt marshes, often so abundant that it forms carpets.

Distribution along southern and western coasts of Europe, including Britain, and eastwards to south-west Sweden.

Family Apocynaceae

Lesser Periwinkle

Vinca minor

February—June. Light- to dark-purple, five-lobed flowers (sometimes pink or white), with petals twisted to the left in the bud and slightly asymmetrical when fully open; flowers, each 25—30mm across, borne singly along the stems; pollinated by long-tongued insects; fruits are pod-like although in some countries (such as Britain) they are rarely formed.

Form of plant a trailing, evergreen shrublet with sprawling, rooting stems up to 60cm long and short, upright flowering stems; leaves smooth, paired, and lance-shaped, 25—45mm long; perennial.

Habitat woods, hedgebanks, and among rocks, commonly forming a dense cover; often an escape from gardens.

Distribution widespread in southern, central, and western Europe; found in Britain but possibly not native.

Family Boraginaceae

Hound's-tongue

Cynoglossum officinale

May—August. Dull, reddish-purple flowers (rarely white) borne in branched, somewhat coiled clusters; each flower is shaped like a shallow, five-lobed funnel, about 6mm across, with scales closing its throat; the fruits are clusters of four nutlets, each covered with barbed bristles, which become attached to fur or clothing.

Form of plant an upright herb about 60cm high, with rather tough stems and lance-shaped leaves covered by a greyish down of silky hairs; the plant smells strongly of mice; biennial.

Habitat waste places, at the borders of woods, dry grassy areas including downland, especially near the sea; also on established dunes.

Distribution not generally common but widely distributed in Europe except in the extreme north and south.

Comfrey

Symphytum officinale

May—July. Drooping, forked clusters of purplish, dull-pink, or creamy white flowers, each flower with a five-lobed, funnel-shaped corolla about 16mm across; fruits are four shiny black nutlets.

Form of plant a sturdy plant with erect, branched, hairy stems up to 120cm high; leaves somewhat hairy and lance-shaped; lower leaves are 15—25cm long, the upper leaves smaller with their bases running down the stem and forming wings; perennial.

Habitat damp, shady places, especially by streams and rivers; in lowland and hilly areas up to 1500m.

Distribution quite common in much of Europe, becoming rare in the extreme south; found as far north as Scandinavia but probably not native.

Family Solanaceae
Woody Nightshade
Solanum dulcamara

May–September. Small clusters of drooping, dark-purple flowers (rarely white) appearing bicoloured because of a prominent central cone of five yellow anthers; flowers about 15mm across, with five narrow petal lobes (later curving backwards) each with two small, green spots at the base; the ripe fruits are small, red berries.
Form of plant a straggling, woody plant with weak stems growing up to 2m and climbing among other plants; leaves are up to 8cm long, the upper ones spear-shaped, the lower ones heart-shaped, arrow-shaped, or pinnately lobed; perennial.
Habitat damp hedges and thickets, river banks, waste places, shingle beaches; up to 1700m.
Distribution common throughout Europe except the extreme north.

Family Scrophulariaceae
Foxglove
Digitalis purpurea

May–September. Handsome, drooping, thimble-shaped flowers borne to one side of a long spike; each flower is 4–5cm long, pinkish purple outside shading to white inside with deep-purple spots, or white outside with purple spots inside; a vigorous spike may bear up to eighty flowers.
Form of plant a rosette of large, undivided basal leaves grows in the first year; from its centre arises the flowering stem in the following year; the stem varies from 50–150cm high; stem and leaves are greyish with soft hairs; biennial.
Habitat open woodland and scrub, heaths, dry hillsides, and mountain rocks, almost always on acid soils, sometimes on light, dry, burnt soils.
Distribution common throughout western Europe; not found in Switzerland or Italy.

Family Lentibulariaceae

Common Butterwort

Pinguicula vulgaris

May–July. Long-spurred, five-lobed, violet-purple flowers, solitary, on slender, leafless stalks up to 18cm high; each flower two-lipped, about 12mm across, with a white-blotched throat; lower lip considerably wider than the upper.
Form of plant a rosette of fleshy, yellowish-green leaves, 2–8cm long, almost oblong in shape, with inrolled edges; a sticky glandular secretion gives the leaf surface a frosted appearance, if small flies alight they are held and then slowly digested by the plant; perennial, passing the winter as a bud.
Habitat bogs, fens, wet heaths, and upland grassland, among wet rocks; up to 2300m.
Distribution quite common in northern, western, and central Europe, restricted to mountains in the south; in Britain absent from southern counties.

Family Verbenaceae

Vervain

Verbena officinalis

June–October. Small, pinkish-mauve flowers in long very slender spikes borne at the ends of stiffly erect stems; each flower is about 4mm across, with five spreading corolla lobes; flowers crowded together but fruits more widely spaced because of continued growth of the spike; attractive to bees, butterflies, and hoverflies.
Form of plant a slender herb with several stiff, erect stems, branching above and growing up to 100cm high; lower leaves deeply pinnately lobed, upper leaves smaller and three-lobed; stems and leaves bearing bristly hairs; perennial.
Habitat waysides, dry waste places; in lowland and hilly areas up to 1500m.
Distribution rather uncommon but found in most of Europe as far north as Britain and Denmark.

Family Labiatae

Black Horehound

Ballota nigra

May–September. Two-lipped flowers clustered in dense whorls at the ends of the branches; each flower has a prominent three-lobed lower lip and a hairy, slightly hollowed upper lip; the petal bases are united forming a tube which has a ring of hairs inside and which is hidden within the joined sepals; visited mainly by bees.

Form of plant a branched, rather straggling herb with an offensive and foetid smell, particularly when crushed; stems up to 100cm high, with downy wrinkled leaves in alternating pairs; perennial.

Habitat waste ground, roadsides, and hedgebanks.

Distribution common throughout Europe; one subspecies is rare in the north but more common in Mediterranean areas.

Ground Ivy

Glechoma hederacea

March–June. Bluish-purple to violet flowers (rarely pink or white), 15–20mm across, in whorls of three to six in small, leafy clusters; the flowers are two-lipped, the lips joined at the base to form a tube, the lower lip larger, heart-shaped, and marked with purple spots; a few flowers may be smaller and without stamens; pollinated mainly by bees.

Form of plant a strongly aromatic, trailing herb with leafy rooting stems and upright flowering stems 10–30cm high; the small, kidney-shaped leaves have long stalks and are borne in pairs, their margins indented with small, rounded teeth; perennial.

Habitat waste ground, hedgebanks, woodland, and grassland, usually on more moist and heavy soils, often forming carpets.

Distribution common throughout most of Europe.

Red Dead-nettle

Lamium purpureum

March–October, sometimes all the year. Small, pale to dark pinkish-purple flowers clustered in dense, leafy whorls at the ends of the stems; each flower is 10–15mm across and two-lipped, joined at the base to form a tube with a ring of hairs within; the upper lip hooded and hairy outside, the lower lip three-lobed.

Form of plant a small, spreading herb with hairy, leafy four-angled stems; long-stalked, heart-shaped, purplish leaves with toothed margins in pairs along the stems; annual.

Habitat waysides, walls, waste places, cultivated ground including gardens where it can be a very common weed; in lowland and upland areas, to 2475m.

Distribution common throughout most of Europe but restricted to mountains in the south.

Corn or Field Mint

Mentha arvensis

July–October. Small, pale-mauve, four-lobed flowers (sometimes white, rarely pink) in dense whorls widely spaced along the stems, each whorl associated with a pair of toothed leaves.

Form of plant branched or unbranched, leafy four-angled stems growing to 60cm high; leaves up to 6·5cm long, rounded or oval with toothed edges; stems and leaves hairy and with an aromatic odour, unlike that of most mint plants, variously described as unpleasant or sickly; very variable in degree of hairiness, leaf form, and number of flowers; perennial.

Habitat cultivated fields, waste places, paths, woodland clearings, ditches and marshy areas; up to 1800m.

Distribution usually common in most of Europe.

Wood Woundwort

Stachys sylvatica

June–October. Reddish-purple (rarely pale-pink or white) two-lipped flowers arranged in whorls of six to ten in a terminal spike; the flowers are about 14mm across, hairy outside and with a ring of hairs inside; the lower lip bears a number of white blotches; flowers pollinated by bees.

Form of plant an upright, branched herb with leafy, four-angled stems up to 120cm high; leaves are long stalked and heart-shaped, with strongly toothed margins; stems and leaves hairy, smelling unpleasant when bruised; perennial.

Habitat hedgebanks, woods, and shady waste places, on the more fertile soils; grows up to 1700m.

Distribution common in most of Europe but rare in the Mediterranean region.

Wild Thyme

Thymus serpyllum

April–September. Small, rose-purple (sometimes pink), two-lipped flowers crowded together in rounded or elongate clusters at the ends of leafy flower stems; pollinated by various insects.

Form of plant a small shrublet with spreading, much-branched, slightly woody stems reaching up to 50cm in length and forming a low-growing mat; from these branches arise rows of upright, hairy flower-stems, usually not more than 10cm high, with pairs of tiny oval leaves having margins fringed with hairs; aromatic, especially in hot weather; an extremely variable species chiefly in the shape and hairiness of stems and leaves; perennial.

Habitat dry grassland, sandy heaths, sand dunes, open woods, and scrub; up to 3300m.

Distribution common in most of northern Europe.

Family Rubiaceae

Field Madder

Sherardia arvensis

May–October. Tiny, pale-mauve, four-lobed flowers in tight clusters of four to eight at the ends of stems and branches, each cluster surrounded by eight to ten long, leafy bracts.

Form of plant a small herb, with a number of spreading, four-angled stems up to 40cm long, branched or unbranched; leaves under 2cm long, narrow and pointed, and borne in widely spaced whorls of four to six along the stems; the leaf margins and underside of the midrib prickly; annual.

Habitat waste places and cultivated fields.

Distribution a common plant (although often unnoticed because of its small size and sprawling stems); probably originally from the Mediterranean region but now widespread throughout Europe and most other temperate regions.

Family Dipsacaceae

Wild Teasel

Dipsacus fullonum

July–September. Small flowers (sometimes white) growing in large, conical, bristly heads and opening in irregular patches; each head up to 8cm long and surrounded by long, spiny bracts; the flowers are visited by bees and long-tongued flies; the dead flowerheads persist throughout the winter.

Form of plant in the first year a rosette of basal leaves is produced; in the second year these leaves die and a stout, leafy, prickly flower stem grows, reaching 50–200cm; the paired stem leaves join at the base, forming a water-holding cup; biennial.

Habitat ditches, stream banks, roadsides, rough pastures, and waste places, especially on clay soils.

Distribution quite common in much of Europe, but not in the far north or south.

Field Scabious

Knautia arvensis

May–October. Attractive, domed heads of up to 4cm across with about fifty bluish-mauve flowers, the largest at the outside having the four petals in two lips; beneath each head is an involucre of two rows of broad, leafy bracts.
Form of plant upright stems up to 100cm high, branched and with the lower parts covered with downward-pointing bristles; basal leaves often toothed and lance-shaped, forming a rosette which persists through the winter, stem leaves usually pinnately lobed with a very large terminal leaflet; very variable especially in leaf form; perennial.
Habitat dry, grassy fields, cornfields, downland, waysides; in lowland and hilly areas; up to 2000m.
Distribution not uncommon, found throughout most of Europe.

Devil's-bit Scabious

Succisa pratensis

June–October. Many small florets together in long-stemmed, semirounded heads each about 2cm across; the florets are mauve to dark blue-purple (rarely pink or white), each with a small, four-lobed corolla from which protrude five purplish-red stamens; in some heads the florets are imperfect, with small, white, non-functional stamens; beneath each flowerhead are two to three rows of leafy scales with additional purple-tipped scales between the florets; pollinated by bees and butterflies.
Form of plant a slender, little-branched herb with upright stems 15–100cm high; basal leaves elliptical forming a rosette, stem leaves fewer and smaller; stems and leaves hairy; perennial.
Habitat damp woods, meadows, and marshes; up to 2400m.
Distribution usually common in most of Europe.

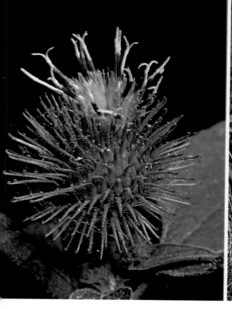

Family Compositae

Great Burdock

Arctium lappa

July–September. Florets in rather flat-topped, yet rounded flowerheads about 3·5cm across; each head borne on a long stalk and surrounded by a large number of stiff, hooked bracts, the heads in numerous small clusters; the florets are visited by long-tongued insects — bees, butterflies, and moths; when ripe, the small fruits are dispersed as a group by the hooked bracts catching in fur or clothing.

Form of plant a vigorous, much-branched herb reaching 130cm high and bearing large, somewhat heart-shaped leaves on reddish stems; each leaf is covered below with greyish, cottony hairs; biennial.

Habitat waysides and waste places, occasionally in open woodland.

Distribution widespread in Europe as far north as southern Norway.

Sea Aster

Aster tripolium

July–October. Flowers (actually flowerheads) rather like a Michaelmas Daisy, with rays which are blue-purple to almost white and which may even be absent, the central florets yellow; flowerheads are up to 20mm across, borne in open, branched clusters; each flowerhead is surrounded by a few, narrow bracts; within these the fruits later develop, each with its parachute of soft hairs.

Form of plant the erect, robust stems grow to 100cm and bear long, narrow, fleshy leaves; stems and leaves are hairless; perennial.

Habitat essentially a salt-marsh plant where is may be found growing even when well covered with mud, also on cliffs and among coastal rocks.

Distribution common on most European coasts.

Musk Thistle

Carduus nutans

May–September. Large, drooping, reddish-purple flowerheads of small, densely packed florets are borne, usually singly, at the tips of spiny, leafy stems; characteristically the upper parts of these stems are bare of both spines and leaves; each head is surrounded by a rather ornamental involucre of stiff-pointed, purplish bracts, the outer ones bent back; the flowerheads emit a somewhat musky odour and are attractive to butterflies and moths, bees, and hoverflies.

Form of plant vigorous, spiny, winged stems up to 100cm bearing deeply cut, spiny leaves; all parts covered with cottony white hairs; biennial.

Habitat waste places, waysides, and fields on limy soils.

Distribution found throughout Europe including the far north, and may be locally common.

Creeping Thistle

Cirsium arvense

June–September. Flowers grouped into either male or female flowerheads 2·5cm across which are always on separate plants; male flowerheads are spherical with an involucre of rather short, purplish bracts; female heads are egg-shaped, with long bracts, and give rise to many tiny, plumed nutlets; the flowers are lilac or greyish-purple, smelling of nectar and attractive to insects.

Form of plant a number of upright stems are produced from creeping, underground roots; the stems may be short or as much as 150cm tall and bear sharply spiny, lobed leaves often very varied in shape; perennial.

Habitat waste places and fields, where it can be a troublesome weed.

Distribution abundant throughout Europe.

Purple Fleabane

Erigeron acer

May–September. Small, almost tubular flowerheads in long-stalked open clusters at the top of the stem; flower-heads 12–18mm across, with a number of narrow, purplish bracts which partly hide the slender florets; central florets small and yellowish, surrounded by short, upright, dull bluish-purple ray florets; fruits are small nutlets, each with a long tawny pappus.

Form of plant an erect herb with a rough, reddish stem 10–60cm high (sometimes reaching 100cm); basal leaves stalked and lance-shaped, form-ing a rosette, stem-leaves narrower; very variable, with several subspecies; annual or biennial.

Habitat dry, sandy, or stony places (including screes, walls, and sand dunes); alpine forms up to 2300m.

Distribution throughout most of Europe, sometimes locally common.

Saw-wort

Serratula tinctoria

July–October. Reddish-purple flower-heads (sometimes white) 1·5–2cm across, singly or in small clusters; florets small and apparently similar, each with a shaggy, spreading corolla, but actually either male or female in separate flowerheads, female heads larger; each flowerhead surrounded by many overlapping, purplish bracts.

Form of plant a slender, rather wiry, branched stem, up to 90cm, more or less erect and leafy; leaves 12–25cm long, varying from deeply, pinnately cut, and toothed to almost undivided, the margins with fine bristles; perennial.

Habitat open grassland, copses, and woodland clearings especially on moist, limy soils; mostly in lowland areas but a smaller, alpine, variety grows between 1600 and 2400m.

Distribution not common but found throughout most of Europe.

Family Alismataceae

Common Water-plantain

Alisma plantago-aquatica

June—September. Delicate, three-petalled pale lilac-purple flowers (sometimes pinkish-white) in an open, much-branched inflorescence; the flowers are short-lived, about 1cm across, opening only in the afternoon.
Form of plant a robust herb up to 100cm high, with smooth, sparingly branched stems and long-stalked leaves; the leaves may be of three kinds — those above the water are large (the leaf blade up to 20cm long) and oval, with conspicuous parallel veins, thus somewhat resembling the un-related plantains, at water level the leaves may be circular and floating or reduced to a small, narrow leaf blade; perennial.
Habitat margins of slow-moving rivers, canals, ditches and ponds, in shallow water, or wet ground.
Distribution common throughout most of Europe.

Family Liliaceae

Meadow Saffron

Colchicum autumnale

August—October. A large, pale-purple flower with a long, slender tube opening out into six petal-like lobes; resembles a crocus but has six instead of three stamens; the fruit emerges above ground in the following spring.
Form of plant usually three leaves — up to 30cm long — glossy, bright green, and parallel-veined, grow from a large underground corm; they appear in spring, dying down in summer before the flower opens; both corm and flower are poisonous; perennial.
Habitat damp meadows and woods often on limestone, usually in large numbers; reaching 2000m in mountain areas.
Distribution rather local but found in many parts of central and south-east Europe, also in Britain and Denmark.

Family Iridaceae

Purple Crocus

Crocus albiflorus

February—May. Flowers like slender trumpets (sometimes white) appearing with the leaves in spring; each flower opens to display six petal-like segments at the top of a long, narrow tube, three prominent yellow stamens, and a central, deep-orange, branched style.

Form of plant tufts of two to four long, narrow, channelled leaves with a conspicuous white midrib; flowers and leaves developing from a fleshy, underground, somewhat saucer-shaped stem (corm) covered by light-brown, fibrous scales; perennial.

Habitat meadows and pastures in lowland and upland areas.

Distribution not common but found in central Europe across to Italy and the Balkans; naturalized in many parts of Britain but never abundant.

Family Orchidaceae

Early Purple Orchid

Orchis mascula

April—June. Reddish-purple to violet flowers (sometimes pink or white), six to thirty together in a loose spike, both bracts and stem decidedly purplish; each flower is about 30mm across, with a large, three-lobed lip mottled with lighter and darker shades of purple and a long, often upturned spur; the flowers on some plants have a strong odour of cats, especially in the evening, while others are sweet scented or even scentless.

Form of plant the stout flower stem grows 15–60cm high, arising from a tight rosette of narrow, usually purple-spotted leaves; perennial.

Habitat woods and other shady places, pastures and grassy slopes usually on limy or clay soils; up to 2650m.

Distribution common throughout Europe except the far north.

Family Polygalaceae

Common Milkwort

Polygala vulgaris

May—September. Rather dense, terminal spikes of ten to forty flowers (also pink, purplish, or white); each flower 6—8mm across, with five sepals, the three outer green and the inner two larger and coloured purple; of the three petals the lowest bears a crest of tiny, strap-shaped segments.
Form of plant a small herb, not more than 35cm high, the stems bearing many small, scattered, narrow leaves of which the uppermost ones are the longest (reaching 35mm); extremely variable; perennial.
Habitat heaths, dry pastures, and other grassy places especially on chalky soils, established sand dunes; some varieties in scrub and on hillsides growing as much as 2200m above sea-level.
Distribution common in most of Europe.

Family Linaceae

Perennial Flax

Linum perenne

May—August. Dainty, powder- or sky-blue flowers with delicate petals which fall shortly after opening; the flowers vary between 15 and 35mm across, with all parts in fives, and are borne in loose clusters on wiry stems.
Form of plant a slender herb, smooth and rather bluish-green, with stems 10—60cm high; the small leaves are numerous, very narrow, single-veined, and stalkless; a very variable species differing in habit, leaf size, and flower shape and size; perennial.
Habitat dry grassland and stony places usually on limestone or chalk; in mountainous regions may be found up to 2280m.
Distribution a rather uncommon plant of central and eastern Europe but with subspecies extending to other regions including Britain.

Family Geraniaceae

Meadow Cranesbill

Geranium pratense

June—September. Large, attractive, cup-shaped flowers of a soft, violet-blue shade, usually paired; the five broad petals alternate with narrow sepals which appear reddish because of numerous red-tipped hairs; the smooth, beaked fruit splits into five single-seeded segments after which the seeds are violently ejected.

Form of plant a softly hairy herb up to 80cm high, the upper stems bearing glandular hairs like those on the sepals; the basal leaves are long-stalked and palmately cut into five to seven deeply divided segments; stem leaves are smaller, more feathery and nearly stalkless; perennial.

Habitat generally on limy soils; found up to 1900m.

Distribution fairly common in northern and central Europe but rare in the extreme north and south.

Family Umbelliferae

Sea Holly

Eryngium maritimum

June—September. Small flowers growing in dense, rounded, prickly heads about 2cm across; at the base of each head are three spiny, leafy bracts; fruits small and hooked.

Form of plant a stiff, blue-green, strongly spiny herb looking rather like a thistle; stems up to 60cm high, with spiny, palmately lobed leaves up to 12cm across; the leaves superficially resemble those of the totally unrelated Holly but differ in shape and colour; leaves of the Sea Holly are blue-green with a dull bloom over the surface; perennial.

Habitat sandy and shingly seashores.

Distribution not uncommon in all coastal areas of Europe.

Family Gentianaceae

Marsh Gentian

Gentiana pneumonanthe

July–October. Large, handsome, five-lobed, trumpet-shaped flowers (sky-blue with five broad-green stripes outside, clear blue within) usually singly or paired at the tops of the flower-stems but sometimes as many as seven together in a leafy cluster; pollinated by bumble-bees which visit the flowers for nectar.

Form of plant a low-growing herb, not more than 40cm high, with a few unbranched stems but sometimes growing in a tuft; leaves narrow, undivided and up to 4cm long; perennial.

Habitat wet heaths, marshy meadows, and bogs, always on acid soils; grows up to 1500m.

Distribution rare although found in scattered areas throughout much of Europe from Scandinavia to northern Spain and Portugal and eastwards to Italy.

Family Boraginaceae

Small Bugloss

Anchusa arvensis

April–September. Small, five-lobed, tubular flowers in forked, leafy clusters, bright blue when open, pinkish in bud; five white, hairy scales close the mouth of the tube, which is sharply bent, and are a distinctive feature of this flower, fruit four small nutlets surrounded by the calyx.

Form of plant all parts of the plant (except the petals) rough and bristly; stems up to 60cm high bear lanceolate leaves with toothed, wavy margins; upper stem leaves partly clasp the stems; rather variable; annual or biennial.

Habitat fields, waste places, and sandy heaths, on light and chalky soils near the sea; also on established sand dunes; inland sometimes on acid soils, reaching 1700m in upland areas.

Distribution often locally common, found in most of Europe.

Common Forget-me-not

Myosotis arvensis

April—October. Attractive, small, bright-blue flowers, each about 4mm across, in slender spikes which are coiled when young, straightening as the flowers open; the buds are pink, changing to blue on opening; the five petals are joined to form a short tube with a bright-yellow eye.

Form of plant a small, hairy herb with branched stems up to 60cm high; the basal leaves are oval, up to 8cm long and form a rosette, stem leaves are lance-shaped; very variable in habit; annual or biennial.

Habitat waste places, cultivated ground, roadsides, hedgerows, woods, and established sand dunes; up to 2000m.

Distribution common and widespread throughout Europe.

Family Scrophulariaceae

Germander Speedwell

Veronica chamaedrys

March—July. Bright-blue, four-lobed flowers, each about 1cm across and with a prominent white eye; flowers borne ten to twenty together, on long stalks in open spikes usually not more than 12cm long.

Form of plant sprawling leafy stems 20—40cm long which turn up at the ends and root at intervals; the paired leaves are dull green and hairy, short-stalked, oval to triangular in shape with coarsely toothed edges; the stems are also hairy but characteristically the hairs are in two lines on opposite sides, changing sides between each pair of leaves; somewhat variable; perennial.

Habitat hedgebanks, woods and clearings, fields, paths, cultivated land; up to 2270m.

Distribution common throughout most of Europe.

Family Labiatae

Common Bugle

Ajuga reptans

April—July. Small, irregular flowers
(sometimes white or pink) arranged in
leafy whorls along the flowering stems;
the uppermost leaves are bluish and
shorter than the flowers; each flower
has an obvious three-lobed lower lip
but the upper lip is almost unnotice-
able; a ring of small hairs lies within
the throat.
Form of plant from a rosette of oblong
leaves grow both upright unbranched
flowering stems 10—30cm high and
also creeping rooting stems; flowering
stems square sectioned, often somewhat bronze and with hairs on only
two opposite sides; perennial.
Habitat grassy places and open woods
in upland areas.
Distribution common throughout
Europe (up to 2000m) from Scandinavia and northern Russia to Portugal,
Sicily, and Greece.

Meadow Clary

Salvia pratensis

May—August. Attractive, tapering
spikes of distinctly two-lipped flowers
(sometimes purple, rarely pink or
white), in few-flowered whorls widely
spaced along the flower stem; each
flower is 1·5—2·5cm long, the lower
lip obviously three-lobed, the upper
lip arched and hooded with long
projecting style and stamens; the two
stamens each have a lever-like projection which, if gently touched, swings
the pollen-covered anther downwards,
thus ensuring successful pollination
by visiting bees; some plants have
smaller flowers without stamens.
Form of plant a hairy, aromatic herb
with leafy stems up to 100cm; leaves
wrinkled, oval to heart-shaped, mostly
long stalked; perennial.
Habitat dry grassland, usually on chalk;
up to 1920m.
Distribution in much of Europe but
rare.

Family Campanulaceae

Harebell

Campanula rotundifolia

May–November. Bell-shaped, five-lobed flowers (sometimes white) about 18mm across growing singly or in loose clusters on slender wiry stalks; the flowers are upright in bud but hang downwards when open.

Form of plant slender, more-or-less upright stems about 40cm high bear a few long, narrow leaves; the long-stalked basal leaves are kidney-shaped and appear only in winter and spring, shrivelling before the flowers appear; perennial.

Habitat heaths, chalk grassland, open woodland, established sand dunes, screes and rocks; especially on poor soils.

Distribution generally common where found, growing throughout Europe as far north as Norway (but not in the Channel Islands) and at altitudes of up to 2150m.

Sheep's-bit

Jasione montana

May–September. Small flowers (rarely white), each with five slender petal lobes, in terminal heads up to 35mm across with a leafy involucre at the base; resembles a scabious but can be distinguished by having the anthers of the stamens joined together; also not unlike one of the Compositae but has a two-celled ovary.

Form of plant upright, usually branched stems 5–50cm high, with undivided, hairy leaves; basal leaves stalked, oblong and forming a rosette, stem leaves much narrower and stalkless; all parts with a disagreeable smell if bruised; usually biennial.

Habitat dry grassy places, heaths, sea cliffs, sometimes on shingle; always on lime-free soils.

Distribution variable — common in some areas, restricted in others; found throughout most of Europe.

Family Compositae

Cornflower

Centaurea cyanus

May–August. Long-stemmed flower-heads about 2·5cm across, with two distinct kinds of floret; the outer florets are bright blue, with a distinctly five-rayed structure; the inner florets are rather inconspicuous, reddish-purple and fertile; the whole flowerhead is surrounded by overlapping brownish-toothed scales.

Form of plant an erect, branched herb with wiry, grooved stems up to 90cm high; upper leaves are small and slender, basal leaves larger and usually lobed; stems and leaves appear greyish because of a covering of soft, cottony hairs; annual or biennial.

Habitat waste places and cultivated areas including cornfields, where it was formerly a common weed.

Distribution found chiefly in lowland areas throughout most of Europe.

Chicory

Cichorium intybus

June–October. Large, blue flower-heads (sometimes pink or white) up to 4cm across and borne directly on the stems; the florets are all strap-shaped and five-toothed, and are surrounded by slender, green bracts; the flower-heads are visited by bees and hoverflies and open in the early morning, closing shortly after noon.

Form of plant a somewhat stiff and untidy herb with branched, leafy, angled stems up to 120cm high; the lower leaves are pinnately lobed, the upper leaves slender and clasping the stem; stems and leaves are usually covered with rough hairs; perennial.

Habitat grassy and waste places also roadsides, usually on chalky soils.

Distribution locally common throughout lowland areas of Europe.

Family Liliaceae

Bluebell

Endymion non-scriptus

April—June. Fragrant, bell-shaped flowers (rarely pink or white) borne to one side in drooping spikes; each flower is associated with two bluish bracts and has six petal-like segments which curl back at the tips revealing six creamy stamens within.

Form of plant the flower stems grow up to 50cm and are surrounded by long, strap-shaped, glossy leaves which often lie on the ground in a rosette; stems and leaves develop from a white underground bulb; all parts exude a sticky, whitish juice when broken; perennial.

Habitat woodland, scrub, and hedgerows, usually in large numbers forming extensive blue carpets; often appearing in abundance following the felling or coppicing of woodland.

Distribution common throughout west and south-west Europe.

Family Orchidaceae

Bird's-nest Orchid

Neottia nidus-avis

May—August. A many-flowered spike of yellowish-brown flowers borne on a robust brownish flower stem 20—50cm high; each flower has five small, petal-like segments and a long, darker-brown lower lip divided into two prominent, spreading lobes; pollinated by small, crawling insects which are attracted by its rather sickly odour.

Form of plant a saprophyte which lives on decaying matter and is completely lacking in chlorophyll; the flower stem grows up from a tangled mass of short, thick, fleshy roots (hence the common name) and bears a number of brownish scales; perennial.

Habitat shady woods especially of beech, but also of oak, birch and pine, usually on chalky soils; up to 1700m.

Distribution relatively common throughout Europe.

Family Ranunculaceae

Marsh Marigold

Caltha palustris

March—August. Flowers large and showy, resembling an oversized buttercup and up to 5cm across, but with no green sepals; visited by a number of insects for nectar and also for pollen from the many stamens; the fruits are conspicuous, clustered pods.

Form of plant typically stout, upright stems about 45cm high with large, glossy, kidney-shaped leaves, but in northern regions and also on mountains the plant is smaller, with slender trailing stems; perennial.

Habitat typically marshy places including sides of streams and lakes, fens, damp woodland, but not in peaty bogs.

Distribution common throughout Europe, including mountain regions up to 2530m, and as far north as Iceland and arctic Russia.

Meadow Buttercup

Ranunculus acris

April—October. Familiar, bright-yellow flowers (sometimes white) in forked terminal clusters; each flower with five sepals and five shiny petals surrounding numerous stamens and the central ovary; each petal has a small basal nectary; fruits are collections of small, beaked nutlets.

Form of plant the tallest of the common buttercups with a much-branched, hairy stem 15—100cm high; basal leaves long stalked and deeply, palmately lobed — further cut into three-toothed segments; upper stem leaves, stalkless, deeply segmented; extremely variable; perennial.

Habitat meadows and damp, grassy places generally; gullies, damp rock ledges, and among stones and rocks on mountains; up to 2500m.

Distribution common and often very abundant throughout most of Europe except the extreme south.

Lesser Celandine

Ranunculus ficaria

February—May. Glossy, bright-golden star-like flowers, 2–3cm across, solitary at the ends of leafy stems; flowers with three sepals and eight to twelve narrow petals (each having a small nectary at the base) fading to white with age; numerous stamens, sometimes missing; fruits are many small nutlets, sometimes failing to develop.
Form of plant a small herb, up to 30cm, with long-stalked, heart-shaped, dark-green, fleshy leaves; some plants produce small, rounded bodies (bulbils) at the base of the leaves, and underground develop small, club-shaped root tubers; both bulbils and tubers can break off and form new plants; perennial.
Habitat woods, hedge banks, stream sides, and damp, bare ground in lowland and hilly areas.
Distribution common throughout Europe.

Lesser Spearwort

Ranunculus flammula

May—October. Forked, leafy clusters of glossy, buttercup-like flowers, but of a somewhat paler yellow; each flower 7–20mm across, characterized by a central almost dome-shaped ovary within the numerous stamens; fruits are collections of small, beaked nutlets.
Form of plant variable; some plants with erect stems reaching as much as 80cm high, other plants shorter with creeping stems rooting below; all stems slightly branched, grooved, and hollow, sometimes reddish in colour; basal leaves long stalked and narrowly heart-shaped; upper leaves spear-shaped (hence the common name), without stalks and with a number of parallel veins; perennial.
Habitat wet places including watersides, marshes, and ditches.
Distribution never common but widespread in much of Europe rare in the Mediterranean region.

Common Meadow Rue

Thalictrum flavum

May—August. Rather fluffy looking, bright-yellow flowers crowded together in branched, rounded clusters at the end of the stem; the yellow colour is actually due to the twenty-four spreading stamens of each flower as there are no petals and the four creamy sepals drop off as the flowers open; visited by insects in search of pollen but also wind pollinated; fruits are a collection of tiny nutlets.

Form of plant an erect stem 50–120cm high, bearing smooth, much-divided, dark-green leaves; each leaf is divided into three stalked sections which are subdivided into wedge-shaped, paired leaflets; somewhat variable; perennial.

Habitat damp meadows, fens, and watersides.

Distribution quite common and found in most of Europe.

Family Nymphaeaceae

Yellow Water-lily

Nuphar lutea

June—September. Handsome, rounded flowers borne above the water; each flower about 5cm across, with five to six broad, greenish-yellow sepals, numerous shorter petals, each with a nectary, and many stamens; the central ovary is topped by a large, flat disc composed of ten to twenty-five radiating stigmas; when fully open there is a distinct odour of alcohol and this, together with the flask-shaped fruit, gives rise to the alternative common name of Brandy Bottle.

Form of plant an aquatic plant with large, leathery, rounded to oblong, floating leaves and delicate, heart-shaped, submerged leaves; the leaf stalks grow from a thick stem buried in the mud and may be 2–3m long; perennial.

Habitat lakes and sluggish streams; up to 1480m.

Distribution common in most of Europe.

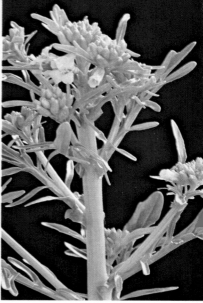

Family Papaveraceae

Greater Celandine

Chelidonium majus

April—October. Flowers 2—2·5cm across in a small, open cluster at the top of the stem; each flower has four spreading petals and numerous stamens which produce abundant pollen; this is collected for food by bees and some kinds of flies; the pod-like fruits contain black seeds, each with a white, fleshy swelling which is eaten by ants.
Form of plant a herb with branched, leafy, brittle stems up to 90cm high; leaves greyish, deeply cut and lobed and almost pinnate in appearance, about 12cm long; a bright, orange-yellow juice is exuded if the stems or leaves are wounded; perennial.
Habitat grassy and waste places, walls, and ruins.
Distribution fairly common throughout Europe.

Family Cruciferae

Common Winter Cress

Barbarea vulgaris

May—August. Bright-yellow, four-petalled flowers, 7—9mm across, densely arranged in a rather broad spike; visited by flies, beetles, and honey-bees; the fruits develop below the young flowers and are erect pods up to 3cm long.
Form of plant a herb with an upright, branched and angular stem 30—90cm high; the basal leaves are irregularly pinnately lobed with a conspicuous, rounded terminal lobe and form a rosette; the uppermost stem leaves are oval and undivided; all leaves are coarsely toothed, dark green, and glossy, and persist throughout the winter; biennial or perennial.
Habitat damp places including stream banks, hedges, and waste places.
Distribution common throughout almost all of Europe.

Black Mustard

Brassica nigra

May–August. Bright-yellow, four-petalled flowers about 14mm across borne in long spikes, the fruits quickly developing below and the flowers in a somewhat flat-topped cluster above; flowers visited chiefly by flies; fruits are four-angled pods, up to 20mm long, held upright and close to the stem; each pod ends in a short beak and contains a number of reddish-brown seeds (the source of table mustard).

Form of plant a branched herb up to 100cm high with stalked leaves; lower leaves bristly and pinnately lobed with a large, rounded, terminal lobe; upper leaves smooth, narrow, pointed, and undivided; annual.

Habitat stream banks and sea cliffs. also waste places and waysides; cultivated.

Distribution widespread in Europe, commonest towards the south.

Family Resedaceae

Wild Mignonette

Reseda lutea

June–September. A dense, conical spike of small, greenish-yellow flowers; each flower has numerous stamens which hang clear of the six, deeply divided petals; unlike Garden Mignonette, the flowers are virtually unscented.

Form of plant an erect, ribbed, and rather bristly stem, very leafy and branched, reaching 75cm or more high; the pinnately cut basal leaves form a rosette which soon withers, stem leaves also have slender pinnate lobes with very wavy margins; rather variable especially in leaf form; biennial or perennial.

Habitat waste and cultivated ground, also rocky places, especially in chalk and limestone regions; up to 2000m.

Distribution not uncommon, found in southern and western Europe and northwards to Britain and southern Sweden.

Family Hypericaceae

Common St John's Wort

Hypericum perforatum

May–September. Terminal, branched clusters of flowers, each flower about 2cm across, the five pointed petals edged and marked with black dots; the five sepals may be similarly marked or sometimes unmarked.

Form of plant erect, rather pale-green, leafy stems vary between 10 and 100cm high; the stems characteristically bear two raised lines; the small, oval leaves, if held up to the light, can be seen to be marked with pale dots (actually oil glands); very variable especially in leaf size and shape; perennial.

Habitat dry grassland, open woodland, scrub, and hedge banks, particularly on chalky soils; up to 2400m.

Distribution common throughout Europe except the far north.

Family Cistaceae

Common Rock-rose

Helianthemum nummularium

May–September. One to twelve five-petalled flowers (sometimes white, pink or orange) in a one-sided cluster, each flower resembling a miniature, open, single rose; the petals may have a small, orange spot at the base; opens in bright sunshine, closing at about midday; if stamens are touched gently they spread out flat against the petals.

Form of plant stems 5–30cm high, short and slender, but tough and sprawling with small, narrow leaves densely hairy beneath; perennial.

Habitat in hilly pastures up to 2800m and in open, dry grasslands on chalk and limestone soils.

Distribution common throughout most of Europe, except the extreme north.

Family Balsaminaceae

Touch-me-not

Impatiens noli-tangere

June–September. Delicate, pendant flowers about 35mm across in small clusters; the first-formed flowers are small and closed, and set seed without the intervention of insects; the other flowers are marked with small, reddish-brown spots and are irregular, with three coloured sepals and petals, the lowest sepal trumpet-shaped, narrowing into a long, curved spur; the fruits open explosively when touched (hence the common name).

Form of plant an elegant, slender herb with smooth, translucent stems 20–180cm high and undivided, toothed leaves up to 12cm long; annual.

Habitat stream sides and moist, shady woods.

Distribution rather uncommon but found in most of Europe except the extreme north and much of the south.

Family Papilionaceae

Kidney-vetch

Anthyllis vulneraria

April–September. Typical butterfly-shaped flowers (sometimes red, purple, or creamy white) in terminal rounded, usually paired heads; a white, woolly calyx surrounds the base of each flower; flowerheads encircled by leafy bracts and in fruit contain numerous, small, one-seeded pods.

Form of plant very variable; spreading stems up to 60cm high with pinnate leaves, the terminal leaflet being the largest; lower leaves often reduced to one leaflet; all parts covered with silky hairs; usually perennial.

Habitat shallow, calcareous, and sandy soils on sunny hillsides, alpine pastures, and dry meadows to 3000m; particularly abundant in chalk and limestone areas, also near the sea; cultivated as a fodder plant.

Distribution general throughout Europe except in the extreme north.

Sweet Milk-vetch

Astragalus glycyphyllos

May–August. Pea-like flowers up to 15mm long, of a yellowish colour varying from creamy white to greenish grey; the flowers, usually in rather dense clusters of up to twenty-five but sometimes as few as five, are visited by bees for nectar; the fruits are curved, pointed pods about 30mm long.

Form of plant a rather stout, spreading herb, often with prostrate, zigzag stems; leaves pinnate with five to six pairs of oval leaflets; perennial.

Habitat sunny open woods, thickets, and rough, grassy places on chalk, limestone, or sometimes gravelly soils.

Distribution uncommon and rather local, found in central and much of northern Europe, but rare in Mediterranean areas.

Dyer's Greenweed

Genista tinctoria

April–September. Golden-yellow, pea-like flowers (about 15mm across) in leafy spikes, visited by a variety of pollen-collecting insects; fruits are pods which explode in dry weather scattering the seeds.

Form of plant a branched, more-or-less upright shrublet 10–200cm high but not usually taller than 70cm; young stems green and slightly hairy, older stems brown and tough; leaves small and lance-shaped; the plant varies considerably in habit, leaf shape, and hairiness; perennial.

Habitat open woods, heaths, and rough pastures on clay and chalk in lowland and upland areas, reaching 1800m.

Distribution quite common in most of Europe but not found in Portugal, Ireland, and some islands.

Horseshoe Vetch

Hippocrepis comosa

May–July. Long-stemmed umbels of five to ten small, pea-like flowers, with upturned standard and small paired wings covering the keel, each flower about 10mm long; the fruits are curved pods up to 30mm long, breaking into several horseshoe-shaped segments; these characteristic fruits (together with the slender, pinnate leaves) distinguish this plant from Birdsfoot Trefoil with which the flowers might be confused.
Form of plant low and tufted with much-branched stems, woody at the base; leaves up to 5cm long with usually three to eight pairs of leaflets; varying in habit also in number and size of flowers; perennial.
Habitat dry, chalky grassland and on cliffs.
Distribution southern, central, and western Europe, including Britain, but never common.

Meadow Vetchling

Lathyrus pratensis

May–August. Yellow, pea-like flowers (up to twelve together) in an open spike, the flowers all turning one way; each flower is 10–20mm across, the standard at the back of the flower streaked with delicate purple markings; fruits are flattened pods.
Form of plant a weak-growing herb climbing over other plants by means of tendrils, with angled stems up to 120cm long; each leaf pinnately divided, the upper three leaflets transformed into tendrils, the lowest pair narrow and leafy; the leaf-stalk is winged with a pair of large, leafy stipules; perennial.
Habitat grassy places including meadows, hedgerows, and scrub; up to 2130m.
Distribution common throughout most of Europe becoming rare in Mediterranean countries.

Birdsfoot Trefoil

Lotus/corniculatus

May–September. Attractive little, pea-like flowers, up to eight together, varying in colour from golden yellow to orange or reddish, and borne in stalked umbels along the stems; distinguished from the rather similar Horseshoe Vetch by the shape of the leaves and pods; the fruits are clustered, straight-sided pods each up to 3cm long.

Form of plant spreading stems up to 40cm long bearing leaves with five-pointed leaflets 3–10mm long, the lower pair close to the stem and resembling stipules; very variable in size and form; perennial.

Habitat pastures and grassy places of all kinds in lowland and upland areas.

Distribution a common plant, widely distributed throughout Europe.

Hop Trefoil

Trifolium campestre

May–September. Tiny, pale-yellow flowers 4–5mm long, clustered, twenty to thirty together, in long-stalked, rounded heads borne along the stems; each head at the base of a leaf; as the flowers fade, the light-brown heads look like miniature hop heads, giving rise to the common name.

Form of plant a downy, sprawling herb with numerous, branched and leafy stems which may reach 50cm long; the trifoliate leaves are short stalked, with widely spaced oval leaflets; annual.

Habitat roadsides, dry pastures, waste, and grassy places; in lowland and hilly areas up to 1715m.

Distribution common throughout Europe except in the extreme north and east; in Britain, abundant in the south but rare in northern Scotland.

Family Rosaceae

Common Agrimony

Agrimonia eupatoria

June—September. A long, slender spike of small, five-petalled flowers much visited by bees for pollen; the base of each flower is grooved, with spreading, hooked bristles; the small fruits are later dispersed by the dry bristles which become entangled in fur, feathers, or clothing.

Form of plant stems reddish, upright, and usually unbranched, growing up to 60cm tall; leaves large and pinnate with saw-toothed leaflets alternately large and small; stems and leaves downy, faintly aromatic when bruised; perennial.

Habitat along roadsides, on waste ground, and in dry sunny pastures; often on limy soils.

Distribution common, especially throughout the northern half of Europe; absent from some Mediterranean areas such as Crete.

Herb Bennet

Geum urbanum

May—September. Small, five-petalled flowers borne on long stalks in open clusters; flowers having five long sepals alternating with five small teeth (this is the epicalyx characteristic of the rose family), also numerous stamens; fruits are clusters of tiny nutlets, each with a long style which remains as a hook, the whole fruit then easily catching in fur or clothing.

Form of plant an erect, downy, somewhat slender, branched herb 20—60cm high; basal leaves pinnately divided; stem leaves more or less lobed or divided, with large, leafy stipules; perennial.

Habitat hedges, thickets, woods, and shady, rather damp places on fertile soils; found up to 1860m.

Distribution common in most of Europe except the far north.

Silverweed

Potentilla anserina

May—August. Long-stalked, solitary flowers borne at intervals along the stems; each flower about 2cm across with five broad petals surrounding the numerous stamens and ovary; outside the petals are five sepals alternating with five large teeth (epicalyx); fruits a collection of tiny nutlets.
Form of plant from a central rootstock radiate a number of rooting, leafy, flowering runners each up to 80cm long; the leaves are handsome, with silvery, silky hairs on the lower or on both sides, pinnately divided into seven to twelve pairs of large, toothed leaflets with tiny leaflets between; perennial.
Habitat roadsides, waste places, damp meadows and other grassy areas, sand dunes; up to 2400m.
Distribution common throughout most of Europe except the south and extreme north-east.

Family Saxifragaceae
Common Saxifrage

Chrysosplenium oppositifolium

March—July. Tiny, greenish-yellow flowers in small, dense, flattened clusters backed by a frill of small, light-green leaves; the coloured part of each flower is provided by four small sepals, the petals being absent.
Form of plant a small herb barely 15cm high with numerous, spreading, leafy stems forming large clumps; the leaves are rounded, 1—2cm across, and borne in pairs along the stems; perennial.
Habitat shady, wet places such as stream sides, among wet rocks and on damp ground beneath trees, often forming spreading carpets; generally on acid soils.
Distribution common in much of Europe, principally the western and central areas, but extending into southern Norway and northern Italy.

Family Umbelliferae

Wild Parsnip

Pastinaca sativa

June—September. Tiny, yellow flowers in stalked clusters (umbels) which are grouped (five to twenty together) in larger umbels, up to 10cm across, at the ends of the leafy stems; visited by flies and beetles attracted by the strong, pungent odour of the whole plant.

Form of plant a robust, hairy herb with ridged and usually hollow stems up to 150cm high; the larger leaves are pinnate with five to nine lobed segments, but beneath the flowerheads the leaves are smaller, less divided and with a broad, sheathing leaf stalk; very variable, with several subspecies; biennial.

Habitat grassy waste places and roadsides, often on chalk or limestone; sometimes an escape from cultivation.

Distribution not uncommon in most of Europe.

Family Monotropaceae

Yellow Bird's Nest

Monotropa hypopitys

June—September. Scented, yellowish-white, waxy flowers later becoming brownish black; flowers bell-shaped, about 15mm across, often with stiff hairs inside, in a short, drooping cluster later becoming erect; this plant could be confused with the Bird's-nest Orchid, which grows in similar habitats but which has two-lipped flowers (the lower lip large and two-lobed) or possibly with a Broomrape which also has two-lipped flowers (the lower lip three-lobed) and which usually grows in grassland.

Form of plant a saprophyte, lacking chlorophyll, with a fleshy, cream stem 8—30cm high bearing scale leaves; perennial.

Habitat damp woods, especially pine and beech, established sand dunes; up to 1800m.

Distribution in most of Europe, never common, rarer in the south.

Family Primulaceae

Yellow Loosestrife

Lysimachia vulgaris

June—August. Terminal, leafy spikes of deep-yellow, cup-shaped flowers blotched with orange inside; the narrow sepals have orange margins; unrelated to Purple Loosestrife despite its name; flower parts in fives or sixes; the flowers, about 15mm across, have two lengths of style (a family characteristic); bees visit for the abundant pollen.
Form of plant a robust herb growing up to 150cm high; the stems bear lance-shaped leaves 5—12cm long, arranged in pairs or in whorls of three or four; the upper leaf surface is dotted with black or orange glands; stems and leaves often downy; perennial.
Habitat lake sides, river sides, and fens, wet often shady places.
Distribution locally common, found almost throughout Europe.

Cowslip

Primula veris

April—May. Sweet-smelling, deep-yellow flowers about 15mm across, drooping to one side in a stalked cluster; flowers funnel-shaped, with five small, notched, petal lobes orange-spotted at the throat; flowers of two kinds (a family characteristic), either having stamens in the throat of the corolla tube and a short style or with the stamens low down in the tube and a long style; this device aids cross-pollination.
Form of plant a rosette of broadly spoon-shaped, wrinkled leaves, each 5—20cm long, with several flower stems up to 20cm high; somewhat variable; perennial.
Habitat meadows on limy or clay soils, also in scrub and open woodland; up to 2200m.
Distribution locally abundant in much of Europe except northern and Mediterranean regions.

Family Solanaceae

Primrose

Primula vulgaris

March—May, sometimes flowering again in autumn or winter. Flowers a delicate greenish yellow (rarely white or purplish), with orange lines around the throat, apparently growing singly on long, pinkish, hairy stalks but actually grouped on a very short flower stem; each flower about 3cm across, with five broad, notched petal lobes; stamens and styles in two different positions (which aids cross-pollination); flowers with stamens deep inside the corolla tube and a long style are termed pin-eyed, those with stamens grouped in the throat and with a short style are thrum-eyed.
Form of plant a rosette of wrinkled, oblong leaves; perennial.
Habitat hedge banks, waysides, railway embankments, open woodland and grassy places; up to 1500m.
Distribution common throughout western and central Europe.

Common Henbane

Hyoscyamus niger

May—September. Large, five-lobed, funnel-shaped, creamy yellow flowers, usually veined with purple and with a dark eye, borne in two rows to one side of the leafy stems; the fruits remain within the toothed calyx and are rounded capsules opening by a lid.
Form of plant an upright branched herb up to 80cm high, the stems and leaves covered with long, sticky hairs; all parts highly poisonous, with a strongly disagreeable odour; leaves pointed oval and up to 20cm long; biennial, sometimes annual.
Habitat roadsides, waste places, and disturbed ground, in sandy places near the sea, also on chalky soils; up to 1860m.
Distribution not common — especially in the extreme north — but found almost throughout Europe.

Family Scrophulariaceae

Common Toadflax

Linaria vulgaris

May—October. Attractive spikes of pale-
or bright-yellow flowers each with a
conspicuous orange blotch; each
flower is irregular and two-lipped,
looking rather like a small garden
Antirrhinum but with a long, pointed,
nectar-containing spur at the lower
side of the flower; pollinated chiefly by
bumble-bees; a form with regular,
five-spurred flowers is very occasionally found.

Form of plant erect, usually unbranched flower stems grow up to
80cm high and bear many long, slender
leaves; stems and leaves usually hairless; perennial.

Habitat paths, stony, grassy, and waste
places; up to 1600m.

Distribution common throughout most
of Europe except the far north and
parts of the Mediterranean region.

Great Mullein

Verbascum thapsus

June—August. Flowers in a dense,
club-shaped spike, the bright-yellow,
saucer-shaped corollas conspicuous
against the greyish, woolly bracts and
sepals; each flower 12—35mm across,
with a five-lobed corolla and five
stamens, the upper three having dense
yellowish-white hairs.

Form of plant a stiffly erect, flowering
stem up to 200cm high, sometimes
branched, with long, pointed leaves
running down on to the stems to form
wings; basal leaves in a rosette; all
parts covered with dense, greyish-
white woolly hairs; rather variable;
biennial.

Habitat dry, often gravelly, grassy, and
waste places, scrub; up to 1850m.

Distribution usually common, in most
of Europe except parts of the extreme
north and east.

Family Labiatae

Wood Sage

Teucrium scorodonia

July–September. Curious little greenish-yellow flowers (rarely reddish or white) borne in pairs in stalked, one-sided spikes; the flowers have a tubular corolla with a long, five-lobed lip above which four red stamens project; pollinated by bees.

Form of plant an upright, branched herb, the leafy stems usually up to 50cm high but sometimes twice as tall; leaves wrinkled more or less heart-shaped and with toothed margins; rather variable in flower and leaf form; perennial.

Habitat woodland and scrub, hedge-rows, grassland, heaths, screes, and established sand dunes, on dry rather ᵈ soils; in lowland and hilly areas.

ᵇution found throughout western, !, and southern Europe as far east ᵃnd and Yugoslavia; usually

Family Caprifoliaceae

Honeysuckle

Lonicera periclymenum

June–October. Highly fragrant, two-lipped, tubular flowers in clusters at the ends of the branches; flowers large, creamy white when first opening but changing colour once pollinated to yellowish orange flushed with red outside; the sweet scent is stronger at night and the flowers are visited by long-tongued night-flying moths which suck up nectar from within the base of the tube; pollinated also by bumble-bees and butterflies; fruits are small, red berries.

Form of plant a deciduous, woody climber with sprawling stems which twine clockwise around nearby shrubs, reaching up to 6m; leaves oval and undivided; perennial.

Habitat woodland, scrub, and hedge-rows, sometimes among shady rocks.

Distribution common throughout most of Europe but absent from Finland and Poland.

Family Compositae

Corn Marigold

Chrysanthemum segetum

July—October. Handsome, bright-yellow, daisy-like flowerheads, about 5cm across, each borne singly on a stalk which is thickest just below the flowerhead.

Form of plant a medium-sized herb with upright, more-or-less branched, leafy stems; all leaves fleshy, the upper ones slightly toothed and clasping the stems, the lower leaves with large lobes or teeth and winged stalks; the whole plant is smooth and hairless and an obvious blue-green in colour; annual.

Habitat in cultivated fields on rather acid soils and at one time locally abundant in cornfields, hence the common name.

Distribution probably originated from the Mediterranean region but now widespread throughout Europe as far north as Norway.

Greater Hawk's-beard

Crepis biennis

June—July. Golden-yellow florets in flowerheads 2—3·5cm across, crowded when young but in open, flat-topped clusters as the stalks lengthen; all florets completely yellow; the bracts beneath each head in two rows; inner bracts distinctly hairy on the inside; small, dandelion-like fruits of differing sizes within the same head.

Form of plant an erect herb with a grooved, rough-surfaced stem up to 120cm high; the stem much branched above, often tinged purple below; basal leaves roughly, pinnately lobed, upper leaves also lobed — barely clasping the stem; all leaves roughly hairy; biennial.

Habitat waysides, waste places pastures, and clover fields usually chalky soils.

Distribution not uncommon; c Europe northwards to southerr dinavia.

Smooth Hawk's-beard

Crepis capillaris

June–November. Bright-yellow florets in flowerheads just over 1cm across in open clusters at the tips of the stems; outermost florets often reddish below; strap-shaped bracts; the fruits resemble those of a miniature dandelion but are held within the enveloping bracts until blown away.

Form of plant branched upright stems up to 90cm high; basal leaves of very variable shape but stalked and roughly pinnately lobed, with the lobes pointing backwards; upper leaves narrow, arrow-shaped at the base, and clasping the stem; all leaves are smooth (sometimes slightly hairy); annual.

Habitat waste places, walls, fields, and grassland; a dwarf variety grows on heaths.

Distribution common in most of Europe.

Common Cudweed

Filago vulgaris

June–September. Tiny florets in small flowerheads which are grouped together to form clusters about 12mm across at the ends of the stems and branches; flowerheads with many yellow-tipped bracts, almost hidden among numerous woolly white hairs, but borne above the level of the leaves.

Form of plant a small herb, usually not more than 30cm high, with branched, leafy stems; leaves small, simple, and spirally arranged; stems and leaves have a dense, white covering of woolly hairs; annual.

Habitat waysides, dry pastures, and heaths, usually on acid, sandy soils.

Distribution fairly common in southern and central Europe as far north as Britain and Denmark.

Mouse-ear Hawkweed

Hieracium pilosella

May—September. Distinctive, lemon-yellow flowerheads, the outer florets often reddish below; each head is about 2·5cm across, borne singly on a hairy flower stem 5—30cm or more high; the bracts forming the involucre beneath each flowerhead are slender and hairy, eventually enclosing a number of small, purplish-black nutlets.
Form of plant a low-growing herb with long, leafy, creeping stems arising from a basal rosette; leaves almost spoon-shaped, up to 12cm long, pale green above but white below with a dense covering of star-shaped hairs; very variable in size and degree of hairiness; perennial.
Habitat short, dry grass, heaths, banks, walls, and rocks; up to 3000m.
Distribution common in most of Europe including subarctic regions.

Nipplewort

Lapsana communis

June—October. Small, pale-yellow flowerheads up to 2cm across, containing between eight and fifteen strap-shaped florets, the heads in open, branched groupings at the ends of the stems; the flowerheads close by mid-afternoon and do not open at all in dull weather; each head is backed by a bottle-shaped involucre of narrow bracts which persist after the small fruits have developed.
Form of plant a leafy herb with a branched stem up to 90cm high; the large lower leaves are roughly pinnately lobed with a large diamond-shaped terminal lobe; upper leaves are toothed and undivided; annual.
Habitat walls, waste places, roadsides, hedgerows, clearings, and cultivated fields; often a common weed.
Distribution widespread and common throughout Europe.

Edelweiss

Leontopodium alpinum

June—September. These well-known, alpine, star-like 'flowers' are really clusters of two to ten tiny flowerheads surrounded by five to nine long, white, woolly leaves; the flowerheads are brownish yellow, about 3mm across, containing several minute florets; the tiny fruits each bears a pappus of club-shaped hairs and are wind dispersed.

Form of plant the flower stems are arising from a rosette the stem slightly waste; a stems and tiny grassland; aving a on heaths. which est some pe hair-

Habitat waste grassland; and on heaths.

Distribution commo...

es,
ually
00m.
arly common
Alps, Pyrenees,
Balkan mountains.

Common Fleabane

Pulicaria dysenterica

July—September. Flat-topped flower-heads 1·5—3cm across, with two kinds of floret, both golden yellow; outer (ray) florets long, strap-shaped, and sterile, inner (disc) florets short and fertile; at the back of each flowerhead are several rows of pointed-tipped, woolly bracts; flowerheads clustered at the tops of the stems; visited by many insects, especially flies.

Form of plant a very woolly herb with leafy, somewhat branched stems up to 60cm high; basal leaves oblong, stem leaves arrow shaped and clasping the stem; all leaves toothed and wrinkled, 3—8cm long; perennial.

Habitat marshy places, wet meadows, beside rivers and ditches.

Distribution common throughout much of Europe, as far north as Britain and Denmark.

Common Ragwort

Senecio jacobaea

June–November. Flat-topped clusters of golden-yellow flowerheads which are about 2·5cm across; the tiny disc-florets have both stamens and ovary, and are surrounded by twelve to fifteen strap-shaped ray-florets (all female); below is a bell-shaped involucre of bracts; both types of floret set seed, with smooth or hairy nutlets each with a small parachute of hairs.

Form of plant an upright, branched herb with ridged, leafy stems 30–150cm high; all leaves deeply pinnately lobed, strong smelling, and poisonous to cattle, basal leaves forming a short-lived rosette; the orange-and-black caterpillars of the Cinnabar Moth are often found on the plant; biennial or perennial.

Habitat roadsides, waste places, and neglected pastures.

Distribution relatively common throughout Europe.

Common Groundsel

Senecio vulgaris

January–December. Crowded or sparsely flowered clusters of small flowerheads consisting only of tiny disc-florets, each head surrounded by a two-layered involucre of bracts, the outer with black tips; each of the minute fruits bears a parachute of long hairs, enabling them to be carried away on the wind.

Form of plant a slightly fleshy and leafy, branched stem, usually upright and 8–45cm high; leaves irregularly pinnately cut and lobed, the uppermost leaves simpler in shape; stems and leaves smooth or developing cottony hairs; very variable in size and leaf form; annual.

Habitat waste places and cultivated ground where it may become a common weed; up to 2500m.

Distribution common throughout Europe.

Golden-rod

Solidago virgaurea

July–October. Branched spikes of many small, bright-yellow 'flowers' (actually flowerheads) borne at the top of the stem; each flowerhead 6–10mm across, consisting of a few small, tubular disc-florets surrounded by six to twelve spreading ray-florets; and many slender, greenish-yellow bracts.

Form of plant an erect, often slightly hairy herb with sparingly branched leafy stems 5–75cm high; leaves toothed, the basal leaves broadly lance-shaped, narrowing higher up the stem; very variable in size and shape of all parts; perennial.

Habitat dry woods, scrub, hedgebanks, cliffs, established sand dunes, grassy and rocky places; up to 2800m, the plants of higher altitudes being dwarf with only few flowerheads.

Distribution throughout Europe, often common.

Common Sow-thistle

Sonchus oleraceus

May–November. Loose clusters of pale-yellow flowerheads, each 2–2·5cm across, the florets all strap-shaped and perfect (that is, with stamens and ovary); outer florets tinged with purple beneath; each flowerhead surrounded by bracts; fruitlets in a dandelion-like 'clock'.

Form of plant a stout-stemmed herb with hollow, branched stems up to 150cm high; leaves very variable but all smooth, grey-green, and toothed; basal leaves usually oval, lower stem leaves pinnately lobed with small, basal, ear-like projections (auricles), upper leaves much smaller with long auricles; all parts contain a milky fluid (latex); annual, sometimes overwintering.

Habitat roadsides, waste places, and cultivated land, a common weed; up to 1800m.

Distribution widespread in Europe.

Common Dandelion

Taraxacum officinale

March–November. Familiar, handsome, golden-yellow flowerheads 3.5–5cm across, borne singly on hollow, leafless stems; beneath each head are three rows of bracts, the outer ones bent downwards; florets all strap-shaped and perfect, that is, with stamens and ovary; the plumed fruits in well-known 'clocks', later carried away by the wind. **Form of plant** flower stems arising from a rosette of large, strongly toothed leaves, usually deeply, pinnately lobed; the terminal lobe large, other lobes pointing backwards with tapering tips; below ground is a long, thick tap-root; all plant parts with milky latex; an extremely variable species; perennial.

Habitat roadsides, waste and grassy places, cultivated land; alpine subspecies reaching 3350m.

Distribution extremely common throughout the Northern Hemisphere.

Goatsbeard

Tragopogon pratensis

May–August. Large, golden-yellow flowerheads 4–6cm across, borne singly on long stems; florets all strap-shaped, surrounded by a single row of pointed bracts joined at the base; the flowerhead is conical in bud, on opening the bracts spread out, their points generally extending beyond the florets; flowerheads closing at noon and in dull weather; fruits are nutlets 10–22mm long each with a large parachute of branched hairs, borne in a conspicuous, feathery 'clock'. **Form of plant** a blue-green herb with long, smooth leaves, grass-like in appearance with obvious white veins; flower-stems branched or unbranched, 30–70cm high; habit variable; annual to perennial.

Habitat roadsides, waste and grassy places, sand dunes; up to 2565m.

Distribution found in most of Europe.

Coltsfoot

Tussilago farfara

February—May. Pale, golden-yellow flowerheads 15—35mm across, borne singly on purplish-scaled flower stems 5—15cm high, appearing before the leaves; each head with a few, small, central disc-florets (which are male) surrounded by up to 300 very narrow, strap-shaped ray-florets (female); below the flowerhead is a single row of green or purplish bracts; ripe fruits forming a small 'clock'.
Form of plant long underground stems give rise to flowering stems and later long-stalked, broadly heart-shaped leaves, each 10—20cm or more across; young leaves are covered with cobwebby hairs remaining as a white felt beneath; perennial.
Habitat waste and cultivated land, cliffs and banks (especially on clay); sand dunes, screes, and shingle; up to 2640m.
Distribution common in most of Europe.

Family Liliaceae
Wild Asparagus

Asparagus officinalis

June—September. Small, bell-shaped flowers (sometimes greenish-white) borne singly or in pairs along the stems, male and female flowers on separate plants; female flowers greenish, about 4mm across, male flowers rather larger; fruits are small, red berries.
Form of plant a much-branched feathery herb, either upright or prostrate, with stems 30—150cm high; the apparent leaves are actually small, needle-like stems in clusters; perennial.
Habitat the upright variety grows in grassy and waste places (sometimes escaped from cultivation); the rare prostrate variety is restricted to grassy sea cliffs and sandy shores.
Distribution the upright variety is widely distributed throughout Europe; the prostrate variety grows only along the western coast of Europe from Germany to south-west France.

Family Amaryllidaceae
Wild Daffodil
Narcissus pseudonarcissus

February—June. Resembling the familiar, springtime garden flower but smaller, borne singly at the top of the stem and sheathed by a large, papery bract; six pale-yellow, petal-like segments surrounding a somewhat longer, golden-yellow trumpet (corona) are borne on a rounded, dark-green ovary. **Form of plant** one or more hollow flower stems up to 35cm high with several bluish-green, strap-shaped leaves arising from an underground bulb; the leaves elongate after the flowers die; damaged stems and leaves exude a whitish slime; perennial. **Habitat** damp woods and meadows, riversides, grassy slopes, and rocky places in upland areas; up to 2150m. **Distribution** not widespread but may be locally abundant; in north-west Europe southwards to Spain, Portugal, and Italy.

Family Iridaceae
Yellow Flag
Iris pseudacorus

May—August. Large, handsome, pale- to deep-yellow flowers emerging two or three together from sheathing bracts at the top of a sturdy, branched stem up to 150cm high; all parts of the flower in threes, the outer segments broad and down curved, often brown veined and with an orange blotch near the base, inner segments upright and narrow; in the centre of the flower are yellow petal-like styles which hide the stamens; fruit a large, three-angled capsule. **Form of plant** the stout stems grow from a fleshy rhizome up to 4cm thick; the leaves are pale green, tall, stiff, and sword-shaped; perennial. **Habitat** margins of lakes, rivers, and ditches, marshes and swampy woodland. **Distribution** common throughout Europe.

Family Araceae

Cuckoo Pint

Arum maculatum

April—June. The 'flower' is actually a long, fleshy column bearing minute, unisexual flowers more or less enclosed in a large, pale-green sheath and terminating in a purplish club; pollinated by small insects attracted by the unpleasant odour and temporarily trapped within the sheath; fruit a cluster of orange-red berries.

Form of plant large, long-stalked leaves appear in early spring; the leaf blade is up to 20cm long, arrow-shaped, glossy, and often spotted with purple; all parts of the plant are smooth and rather fleshy; perennial.

Habitat hedgerows, shady banks, and damp woods, tolerates shade well; prefers limy soil.

Distribution common in central and southern Europe, and also as far north as southern Sweden.

Family Menyanthaceae

Bogbean

Menyanthes trifoliata

April—July. Attractive and unusual flowers, rose pink in the bud, which open to show five paler corolla lobes, each thickly fringed with long, white hairs; flowers about 15mm across, in spikes of ten to twenty blossoms.

Form of plant an aquatic herb with flower stems 12—35cm high and glossy, trifoliate leaves, in size, shape, and colour not unlike those of a Broad Bean plant; both stems and leaves held well clear of the water; perennial.

Habitat stagnant waters up to 4m deep, bogs, fens, and ditches; in lowland but more especially upland areas to 2400m.

Distribution often locally common and forming sheets of vegetation, in much of Europe but becoming rarer in the south.

Family Scrophulariaceae

Crested Cow-wheat

Melampyrum cristatum

June–September. A dense, four-sided spike of rather small, purple, yellow-throated flowers which are made conspicuous by their attractive and unusual bracts; each flower is two-lipped and associated with a broad, rose-coloured bract edged with long, fine teeth; the lowest bracts have the tip drawn out into a long, green point; pollinated by bumble-bees.

Form of plant a small herb, not more than 50cm high, with a single, often unbranched, stem and narrow, paired leaves; a semiparasite growing on the roots of other plants; rather variable; annual.

Habitat thickets, margins of woods, dry, grassy, or rocky places; up to 1500m.

Distribution rather rare but found in much of Europe except parts of the north and south.

Common Figwort

Scrophularia nodosa

June–September. Small, dingy, oddly shaped flowers borne in an open, repeatedly forked, leafy cluster; each flower is about 1cm across, on a stalk dotted with tiny glands, and has a small, green, five-toothed calyx and a bulbous, yellowish-green corolla with a purplish-brown upper lip; pollinated mainly by wasps.

Form of plant a tall, unpleasant-smelling herb with four-angled, leafy stems which reach 80–150cm; leaves, 6–13cm long, pointed, oval and toothed; perennial.

Habitat damp, shady places such as woods and hedge banks, also by watersides; in lowland and upland areas up to 1850m.

Distribution quite common and widely distributed throughout most of Europe from Norway to Spain, northern Italy, and Greece.

Family Liliaceae

Fritillary

Fritillaria meleagris

April–May. Handsome, drooping, tulip-shaped flowers 3–5cm across, strikingly patterned in alternating squares of pink and dull purple (sometimes white), usually solitary but sometimes in pairs; within the flower at the base of each of the six petals is a large, glistening nectary; flowers visited by bumble-bees for the nectar.

Form of plant the leafy flower stems grow 20–50cm high; leaves rather blue-green, slender and pointed, not more than six on a stem and 8–20cm long; perennial.

Habitat damp meadows and pastures, occasionally escaping from gardens; where undisturbed it may form extensive colonies.

Distribution northern and central Europe southwards from Britain and Sweden; rather local, becoming rare in many areas through overpicking.

Family Orchidaceae

Frog Orchid

Coeloglossum viride

May–August. Slightly scented, rather inconspicuous flowers in a slender, leafy spike; each flower has three greenish outer segments which form a hood hiding two slender, green inner segments; the long strap-shaped lip is yellowish green to reddish brown, the tip having two obvious lobes with a small tooth between; at the back of the flower is a greenish spur, short, rounded, and containing nectar.

Form of plant the single flower stem is somewhat reddish, unbranched, and 10–35cm high; the basal leaves are oval, stem leaves smaller and slender; all leaves parallel veined; perennial.

Habitat damp woods and hill pastures, often on chalky soils, up to 2700m.

Distribution locally abundant, especially in mountainous areas, in central and northern Europe.

Family Orchidaceae

Coralroot

Corallorhiza trifida

May—August. Slender spikes of two to twelve widely spaced, rather inconspicuous, drooping flowers; each flower has three greenish or yellowish-white segments, two similarly coloured inner segments and a short, grooved lip which is white with characteristic red blotches; the ovary is relatively large and straight.

Form of plant the yellowish, clustered flowering stems grow up to 30cm tall and, except for two long, sheathing scales, are entirely leafless; up to ten such stems arise from the underground rootstock which is branched and coral-like; perennial.

Habitat occasionally established dunes, usually damp, peaty, or mossy woods especially pine, birch, or alder, also beech; grows up to 1820m.

Distribution rather rare but found throughout central and northern Europe.

Lady's Slipper Orchid

Cypripedium calceolus

May—July. Flowers borne singly at tip of long, slender stem; largest and most handsome of the European orchids; the flowers, which are nearly 5cm across, have maroon petals and a large, yellow pouch which is spotted red inside.

Form of plant stems 30—50cm high with large, strongly veined, pointed leaves; perennial.

Habitat in ash, oak, or hazel woods on limestone soils, usually on hill or mountain slopes.

Distribution can still be found in many mountainous parts of Europe, up to about 1700m, including the Pyrenees, Alps, Dolomites, and northern Russia and Siberia; in Britain may be found very rarely in the north of England. Formerly widespread but now overpicked.

Broad-leaved Helleborine

Epipactis helleborine

July—September. Numerous half-drooping, unscented flowers arranged in a leafy, one-sided spike; the number of flowers varies from an average of fifteen to almost 100; each flower is nearly 2cm across, with green to purple outer segments, pinkish inner segments and a small pink and brown rounded lip; both shape and colour of the flowers parts are very variable.

Form of plant usually only one flower stem (up to 80cm high) which bears broad, pointed, oval leaves up to 17cm long, with generally five prominent parallel veins; perennial.

Habitat shaded woodlands but also more open sites such as hedge banks, open hillsides, and even established dunes; often on acid soils; may reach 1500m.

Distribution not common but found throughout Europe.

Fly Orchid

Ophrys insectifera

May—July. A thin spike of well-spaced flowers, the sombre colouring and shape of the inner segments of each flower producing a lifelike resemblance to a large fly; the 'fly' appears to be resting on the three outer segments, which are green and spreading; the lobed lip of the flower forms the 'body', purplish brown and hairy with a shiny blue central patch, and also the 'wings'; the lateral inner segments are slender, dark, and hairy, and resemble paired limbs; flies attempt to mate with the flowers and may effect pollination.

Form of plant leafy flower stems up to 60cm tall; perennial.

Habitat woods and grassy places on limy or clay soils; up to 1850m.

Distribution widespread in Europe, usually rare.

Glossary

annual a plant which flowers and dies within one year.

anther the part of the stamen which produces pollen.

berry a fleshy fruit with numerous, hard-coated seeds.

biennial a plant which takes two years to complete its life cycle, producing leaves in the first year, flowering and then dying in the second.

bract a small leaf, green or scale-like, either at the base of a flower stalk or grouped beneath a flowerhead.

bulb an enlarged, underground bud with fleshy scale leaves.

bulbil a small bud or tuber-like structure formed at the base of a leaf or in place of a flower, which breaks off and grows into a new plant.

calyx a collective name for the sepals either separate or joined.

capsule a dry fruit which splits open releasing the seeds.

compound (of a leaf) divided into separate leaflets.

corm a swollen, flattened, underground stem covered by papery scales.

corolla a collective name for the petals either separate or joined.

deciduous applied to any part of the plant shed at the end of a season, most frequently referring to leaves.

dicotyledon a plant of the major group which is characterized by having two seed leaves, flower parts mostly in fours or fives and usually broad, net-veined leaves.

drupe a fleshy fruit containing one large seed which is surrounded by a stony layer.

epicalyx a circle of small, leafy structures borne outside the calyx.

floret a small flower which forms part of a compound head as in the family Compositae, or in a compact or open inflorescence as in sedges and grasses.

gland a structure outside or within the plant which produces a secretion such as oil or scent.

herb a plant with unthickened, that is, non-woody stems, usually dying down in autumn.

inflorescence the flowers and associated structures on a flower stem; also the pattern of branching of the flower stem.

involucre a group of bracts or other leafy structures developing below the flowers.

irregular describes flowers which are bilaterally symmetrical, that is, which can be cut into equal halves in only one plane, from front to back.

latex a milky juice, white or coloured.

leaflet a separate segment of a leaf which often resembles a leaf but has no associated bud.

lobed divided, but not into separate parts.

monocotyledon a plant of the major group which is characterized by having one seed leaf, flower parts mostly in threes, and usually narrow leaves with parallel veins.

nectary a glandular body within the flower, varying in shape and position, which secretes honey-like nectar.

nutlet a small, single-seeded fruit with a hard coat.

ochrea a delicate sheath encircling the stem just above a leaf.

ovary the central part of the flower containing the ovules which later develop into seeds.

palmate having leaflets radiating from the same point.

pappus a circle of hairs, bristles, or scales (representing the calyx) at the top of the ovary of flowers of the family Compositae.

perennial a plant which lives for more than two years, usually flowering in each year.

petal a segment of the corolla, often brightly coloured.

pinnate bearing leaflets along each side of the leaf axis.

pod a long, dry cylindrical fruit which splits open releasing the seeds.

regular describes flowers which are radially symmetrical.

rhizome a creeping underground stem, often swollen with food reserves, from which grow leaves and stems each year.

rosette a radiating cluster of leaves, usually lying close to the ground.

saprophyte a plant which lacks chlorophyll and lives by absorbing food from decaying organic matter.

scale a papery or woody flap of tissue, usually a much-reduced leaf.

sepal a segment of the calyx, usually small, green, and leaf-like.

shrub a much-branched, woody plant, the branches arising at or immediately above soil level.

shrublet a small shrub usually less than 30cm high.

simple undivided or not compound, usually applied to a leaf which is not divided into leaflets.

spur a long, normally nectar-producing projection from a sepal or petal.

stamen the male reproductive structure, usually stalked.

stigma the receptive part of the ovary, varying in form, on which the pollen germinates.

stipule a lateral outgrowth, paired and varying in shape, which develops from the leaf base.

style a prolongation of the ovary which bears the stigma(s).

tendril a long, sensitive organ, often formed from a leaf, which coils around any object it touches.

trifoliate with three leaflets, as in a clover leaf.

tuber a swollen, underground stem or root.

umbel an umbrella-shaped inflorescence with the flower stalks arising from a common point.

whorl a ring of three or more similar structures.

Index